Tax
Policy
and the Economy volume 1

edited by **Lawrence H. Summers**

NBER and
MIT Press
Journals

226890

339
T 235

Send orders and business correspondence to:
The MIT Press
55 Hayward Street
Cambridge, MA 02142

In the United Kingdom, continental Europe, and the Middle East and Africa, send orders
and business correspondence to:
The MIT Press Ltd.
126 Buckingham Palace Road
London SW1W 9SD England

ISSN: 0892-8649
ISBN: hardcover 0-262-19263-2
       paperback 0-262-69115-9

Contents

Lawrence H. Summers

Harvard University and NBER

Introduction

The past year witnessed one of the most sweeping reforms of the federal income tax system since its inception. Tax policy issues commanded the attention of policy makers, the media, and the public. Although the new tax code enacted in 1986 will not take full effect for several years, attention is already turning to further tax reform efforts. Some observers anticipate the need for new measures to increase revenues. Others see the need to reform the tax system to accommodate ongoing changes in the economy. Tax policy debates will be with us for years to come.

Economic research can make an important contribution to tax policy debates. It can quantify the impact of potential tax changes on economic behavior and can isolate the many indirect effects that tax policies have on economic efficiency and equity. All too often, however, the results of economic tax policy research are not presented in a way that is accessible to policy makers, businessmen, lawyers, and others involved in the formulation of tax policy.

In an effort to communicate research results the NBER is initiating a series of annual conferences and publications on "Tax Policy and the Economy." The current volume is the first in this series. Unlike many other Bureau publications, this series is nontechnical and is written not only for academics but also for the broader tax policy community. Although the papers included here do not endorse particular policies, they provide valuable input for both public and private decision making.

This inaugural issue of *Tax Policy and the Economy* contains six studies of diverse tax policy issues. Each paper brings together new data to examine aspects of an important policy issue. I shall briefly describe each of the papers beginning with Alan Auerbach's and James Poterba's study, "Why Have Corporate Tax Revenues Declined." This paper examines the striking decline in corporate tax revenues as a share of GNP. Corporate tax burdens relative to GNP are only about one-third as great as they were in 1960. Auerbach and Poterba show that less than half of this decline is due to changes in tax rules. Declining corporate profits have had a greater impact on revenue collections than all legislative changes taken together. Even after the 1986 Tax Reform Act is phased in, corporate tax burdens relative to profits will be light by historical standards.

In recent years there has been an increase in share repurchases and mergers. John Shoven's paper, "New Developments in Corporate Finance and Tax Avoidance: Some Evidence," examines the effect of this trend on tax collections. He concludes that these devices have helped and will continue to help corporate shareholders escape the double taxation of dividends. These financial devices may have also cost the Treasury a significant amount of money—perhaps as much as $25 billion in 1985.

In "Amnesty, Enforcement, and Tax Policy" Herman Leonard and Richard Zeckhauser review the experience of several states with tax amnesty programs and consider the likely effects of a federal tax amnesty program. The authors stress that a de facto amnesty already exists, because the IRS currently waives about half the penalties it could collect from delinquent taxpayers. They conclude that a full-scale tax amnesty, coupled with stricter enforcement procedures, would raise revenue in the short run and would enhance future efforts to enforce the income tax by getting more taxpayers on the rolls. However, they caution that there are long-term risks. An amnesty might change attitudes toward the income tax and therefore undermine the voluntary compliance that ensures the success of the current program.

"The 1983 Increase in the Federal Cigarette Excise Tax" by Jeffrey Harris explores the economic effects of tobacco taxation. He considers what effect these taxes have on the market for cigarettes and their ultimate impact on health. In particular, he examines what effect the recent hike in the federal excise tax on cigarettes had on prices. Over the last five years the price of a pack of cigarettes rose by 36 percent (adjusted for inflation). This price increase was much greater than the increase in the tax burden on cigarettes. Harris argues, however, that much of it may nonetheless have been caused by the recent tax increase, since it provided a focal point that facilitated collusion among cigarette producers. Harris finds that the tax increase considerably reduced the number of smokers, and he concludes that it almost certainly avoided a substantial amount of disease.

Douglas Bernheim's study "Does the Estate Tax Raise Revenue?" suggests that the federal estate tax could conceivably reduce federal tax revenues. Because of its many exemptions and the tax avoidance schemes that are legally permissible, the tax raises only a small amount of revenue (approximately $6 billion in 1985). The estate tax also encourages people to take avoidance actions, such as making gifts to their children, that reduce income tax collections. But standard estimates of the revenue raised by the estate tax do not include its negative impact on income tax collections. Bernheim presents data suggesting that the reduction in income tax revenues caused by the estate tax approximately offsets the revenue it generates directly.

The final paper by Michael Boskin and Douglas Puffert shows that the redistributions between married workers and single workers in the Social Security system dwarf the much discussed "marriage tax" effects of the individual income tax. Social Security results in very large redistributions from married women who work to married women who do not, and provides very low rates of return for women who are divorced or widowed. The authors also demonstrate that for many individuals Social Security benefits and contributions are weakly related.

Acknowledgments

The authors and I are indebted to the people at the NBER who made this volume and the conference upon which it is based possible. NBER president Martin Feldstein conceived the idea of starting a series of annual volumes communicating the results of economic research on tax policy to a wide audience, and he has supported this project throughout. Deborah Mankiw administered the organization of the conference and this volume with great skill and good cheer. There would be no volume without her efforts. Kirsten Foss Davis and Ilana Hardesty did a fine job of handling the logistics of the conference itself. Merri Ansara and Jane Konkel typed and retyped the manuscripts under great time pressure. Finally, I am grateful to the authors of the papers presented here, whose research has set a high standard for future volumes in this series.

Lawrence H. Summers

Alan J. Auerbach and James M. Poterba

University of Pennsylvania, Harvard University, and NBER,
Massachusetts Institute of Technology and NBER

Why Have Corporate Tax Revenues Declined?

Corporate income tax revenues have declined dramatically during the
last two decades. The corporate tax accounted for almost 20 percent of
federal receipts during the 1960s, compared with only 7 percent of federal receipts in the last five years. Federal corporate taxes averaged
3.9 percent of gross national product (GNP) during the first five years of
the 1960s, 2.7 percent of GNP for the first five years of the 1970s, and
only 1.4 percent of GNP for the first five years of the 1980s. In 1985, the
tax-to-GNP ratio was less than half what it was ten years ago and only
one quarter as large as in 1955. In 1982, real corporate tax payments were
lower than in any year since 1940. Although corporate taxes in each of
the last three years were substantially greater than in 1982, the average
level of tax receipts remains at its postwar low.

The erosion of corporate tax revenues is widely regarded as the result
of legislative changes. For example, a frequently cited study by McIntyre
(1984) argues that

*The decline of the corporate tax began with the adoption of the investment tax
credit in the 1960s, and continued into the 1970s as Congress adopted one loop-
hole after another in response to corporate lobbyists . . . the largest single blow to
the corporate tax came in 1981 with the passage of . . . the Accelerated Cost Recovery System, which opened up massive new possibilities for corporate tax
avoidance. (p. 1)*

We are grateful to William Gentry for research assistance, to Sandra Byberg (IRS), Ken
Petrick (BEA), Len Smith (Joint Tax Committee), William States (IRS), John Voight (IRS),
and Teresa Weadock (BEA) for data assistance, to Jane Gravelle and Lawrence Summers for
helpful comments, and to the NSF, NBER, and the University of Pennsylvania Institute for
Law and Economics for financial support. This research was completed while the second
author was a Batterymarch Fellow. It is part of the NBER Program on Taxation.

This viewpoint clearly influenced the architects of the recently enacted Tax Reform Act of 1986 (TRA). The new law's stringent corporate minimum tax of 20 percent, coupled with significant reductions in capital recovery allowances, will raise corporate taxes by $120 billion during the next five years.

This paper examines why corporate taxes have declined. It decomposes movements in federal tax receipts into components attributable to changes in tax rates, changes in tax preferences, changes in corporate profitability, and other factors. The results suggest that although legislative changes have been important contributors to the decline of corporate tax revenues, they account for less than half of the change since the mid-1960s. Reduced profitability, which has shrunk the corporate tax base, is the single most important cause of declining corporate taxes.

The paper is divided into five sections. Section 1 documents the decline in corporate tax revenues during the last three decades. Section 2 presents a simple division of changes in corporate taxes into components due to changes in tax rules and changes in the corporate tax base. It shows that during the last twenty years, though the average tax rate has fallen by nearly one third, corporate profitability has declined by a factor of two. Section 3 examines the factors that have been most important in reducing average corporate tax rates. It focuses on changes in capital recovery, inflation-induced misstatement of corporate profits, and various legislative changes. The fourth section examines the expected revenue gains under the TRA and presents preliminary evidence on how the bill will alter average tax rates. There is a brief conclusion.

1. The Withering Corporate Income Tax

The decline in corporate taxes played an important part in stimulating recent calls for tax reform. The withering of the corporate income tax, however, began long before the passage of the Economic Recovery Tax Act (ERTA) in 1981. Corporate tax payments as a share of GNP or the value of corporate assets have been declining for nearly three decades. This trend accelerated during the last five years, when real corporate taxes also declined.

Table 1 presents four measures of the net corporate tax payments by nonfinancial corporations. We measure tax payments net of refunds obtained by carrying current losses back to offset prior taxes, including taxes collected as a result of audits or other retabulations. A detailed description of our data series is provided in the appendix. We focus on nonfinancial corporations (NFCs) because they were most significantly affected by the changes in capital recovery rules under ERTA. The

NFCs accounted for 89 percent of corporate tax revenues in 1984 and 1985, and movements in their tax payments track total taxes very closely. There are also detailed tax provisions affecting financial firms (see Neubig and Steuerle (1983)) that we avoid by focusing on the NFCs.

The first column of Table 1 reports the NFC's real corporate tax pay-

Table 1 FEDERAL CORPORATE TAX REVENUES, 1959–1985

Year	Federal receipts from NFCs ($1986)	NFC federal taxes as a percentage of		
		GNP	Replacement cost of net NFC assets	Federal receipts
1959	73.7	3.94	4.74	21.6
1960	66.7	3.48	4.25	18.5
1961	66.9	3.41	4.22	18.4
1962	67.8	3.28	4.24	17.6
1963	75.0	3.49	4.65	18.3
1964	77.2	3.41	4.74	19.1
1965	85.9	3.58	5.17	20.1
1966	89.5	3.54	5.16	19.0
1967	80.9	3.10	4.38	16.6
1968	92.3	3.40	4.88	17.1
1969	85.9	3.09	4.42	14.9
1970	64.5	2.33	3.21	12.1
1971	67.4	2.36	3.29	12.9
1972	71.3	2.38	3.41	12.5
1973	80.0	2.54	3.69	13.1
1974	75.7	2.42	3.12	12.1
1975	66.4	2.15	2.53	11.6
1976	79.7	2.46	2.96	12.9
1977	83.9	2.47	3.04	12.8
1978	87.7	2.45	3.01	12.5
1979	81.8	2.23	2.66	11.1
1980	70.0	1.91	2.14	9.4
1981	57.3	1.54	1.68	7.4
1982	37.7	0.93	0.98	4.6
1983	47.4	1.26	1.39	6.5
1984	59.5	1.49	1.76	7.7
1985	50.0	1.22	1.51	6.2
Five-year averages				
1961–65	74.5	3.43	4.60	18.7
1966–70	82.6	3.09	4.41	16.0
1971–75	72.1	2.37	3.21	12.4
1976–80	80.6	2.31	2.76	11.8
1981–85	49.6	1.29	1.47	6.5

Data on tax receipts from the nonfinancial corporate sector are based on authors' calculations, which are described in the Appendix. Receipts are net of carryback refunds and audit-induced tax payments.

ments, measured in 1986 dollars. These tax payments peaked at $92.5 billion in 1968, and, with the exception of three years in the late 1970s, they have been substantially below this level ever since. Average tax payments by the NFCs were $78.6 billion in the 1960s, $76.4 billion in the 1970s, and $49.6 billion for the last five years. The data demonstrate the recent decline in corporate tax revenues, however, since average payments for 1976 to 1980 were 63 percent greater than average revenues in the last five years.

This decline in corporate taxes is even more remarkable when viewed in the context of the growing economy. The second and third columns in Table 1 describe corporate taxes relative to GNP and corporate assets. Corporate taxes averaged 3.7 percent of GNP during the 1960s, compared with 1.3 percent during the first half of the 1980s. In 1982, when corporate taxes reached their postwar low, they accounted for only 0.9 percent of GNP. An equally pronounced decline emerges from column 3, which shows the ratio of tax payments by nonfinancial corporations to the net replacement value of their tangible assets. This asset measure is constructed by subtracting corporate debt outstanding from the replacement cost of corporate tangible assets and provides a natural scaling variable for corporate taxes, because it reflects changes in the size of the corporate sector. Tax payments by NFCs averaged 4.6 percent of net assets during the first five years of the 1960s and were even higher at the end of the 1950s. The tax-to-asset ratio has fallen by a factor of 3 during the last twenty-five years. For the five years ended 1985, it averaged 1.5 percent, and it fell below 1 percent in 1982. Taxes as a percent of assets fell by 1.4 percent between 1961–1965 and from 1971–1975 and declined by as much again during the last ten years.

Corporate taxes have also become a substantially less important part of the federal budget. They accounted for 6.5 percent of revenues during the most recent five years. By comparison, corporate taxes were nearly three times as important, accounting for 18.7 percent of federal revenues, from 1961 to 1965. The rapid growth of federal revenues from other sources, particularly social insurance taxes, coupled with declining corporate taxes to explain the pronounced reduction in the corporate tax share during the last twenty-five years.

2. Declining Tax Rates Versus Declining Tax Base

The decline in corporate taxes can be divided into two components: a decline in the rate at which corporate profits are taxed, and a decline in corporate profits themselves. The first component is the average tax rate, which has attracted widespread attention in the tax policy debate of the last five years (see Joint Committee (1984) or Spooner (1986), for example). Many analyses of the corporate tax focus exclusively on the average rate, however, and imply the misleading conclusion that its movements are the sole cause of recent reductions in corporate tax revenues. This section demonstrates that although average tax rates have declined, changes in corporate profits, the base of the corporate income tax, are an equally important factor in explaining the change in corporate taxes.

2.1 EFFECTIVE TAX RATES AND THE TAX-TO-ASSET RATIO

The tax-to-asset ratio is the product of the average tax rate and the corporate profit rate:

Taxes/Assets = (Taxes/Profits)(Profits/Assets).   (1)

Profits denote the real economic profits earned by corporate equity holders,[1] Taxes/Profits is the average effective tax rate, and Profits/Assets defines the real economic profit rate. Profits excludes foreign source income of U.S. corporations, since our asset measure includes only domestic capital. A detailed description of our measure of economic profits is provided in the Appendix.

Table 2 presents data on the tax-to-asset ratio, the average tax rate, and the profit rate for each year since 1959, the year when some IRS data used in our calculations first became available. The data clearly indicate that both falling average tax rates and a decline in profitability have contributed to lower corporate taxes. The average effective tax rate was 41.8 percent during the 1960s, compared with 30.8 percent during the last five years, a decline of more than one quarter. Average tax rates declined throughout the 1970s, averaging 43.4 percent for 1971 to 1975 and 40.1 percent for 1976 to 1980. The average effective tax rate for 1981–1985 was 9 percent lower than its value for 1976–1980. This decline is twice as large as the drop between the first and second halves of the 1970s.

The second column of Table 2 reports the economic profit rate on nonfinancial corporate capital. The profit rate trends down throughout our sample period but drops quite sharply in the 1980s. From an average of

---

1. Alternative views of what constitutes the corporate tax base are also possible. Feldstein and Summers (1979) and Feldstein, Dicks-Mireaux, and Poterba (1983) consider the total earnings of the corporate sector, including those paid to debt holders, as the tax base. Because interest payments are taxed less heavily than equity earnings, measuring the average tax rate relative to this base would lower the average tax rate but not affect its decline over time. The profit rate associated with this concept of corporate profits has also declined significantly during our sample period.

10.9 percent during the 1960s, the profit rate fell to 7.2 percent during the 1970s and 4.9 percent during the last five years. In 1982, when corporate taxes reached their postwar low, the corporate profit rate was also at its lowest level (2.9 percent). Although profits accruing to equity holders have rebounded since then, averaging 6.3 percent in the last two years, they are still well below their level in the previous two decades.

Table 2 THE AVERAGE TAX RATE AND CORPORATE PROFITABILITY, 1959–1985

Year	Average tax rate	Corporate profit rate	Ratio of taxes to NFC net assets
1959	0.50	9.55	4.74
1960	0.51	8.30	4.25
1961	0.48	8.79	4.22
1962	0.42	10.09	4.24
1963	0.44	10.70	4.65
1964	0.41	11.69	4.74
1965	0.38	13.55	5.17
1966	0.38	13.70	5.16
1967	0.38	11.52	4.38
1968	0.41	11.93	4.88
1969	0.43	10.17	4.42
1970	0.45	7.07	3.21
1971	0.41	7.94	3.29
1972	0.41	8.38	3.41
1973	0.43	8.67	3.69
1974	0.50	6.20	3.12
1975	0.42	5.95	2.53
1976	0.43	6.83	2.96
1977	0.38	7.98	3.04
1978	0.38	7.92	3.01
1979	0.40	6.59	2.66
1980	0.41	5.27	2.14
1981	0.36	4.62	1.68
1982	0.34	2.88	0.98
1983	0.32	4.40	1.39
1984	0.28	6.24	1.76
1985	0.24	6.40	1.51
Five-year averages			
1961–65	0.42	10.96	4.60
1966–70	0.41	10.88	4.41
1971–75	0.44	7.43	3.21
1976–80	0.40	6.92	2.76
1981–85	0.31	4.91	1.47

The three columns correspond to Taxes/Profits, Profits/Assets, and Taxes/Assets as described in the text. The third column is the product of the first two. Data descriptions are provided in the Appendix.

This dramatic decline in corporate profits is an important source of lower corporate tax receipts. The last column of Table 2 shows that the tax-to-asset ratio at the beginning of the 1960s, for example, was 3.1 times that at the beginning of the 1980s. The average effective tax rate was 1.35 times its level in recent years, and the profit rate was 2.2 times its recent value. Declining profitability is therefore substantially more important than changes in the average tax rate in accounting for the reduction in corporate taxes.

The relative importance of changes in tax rates and the tax base can be illustrated by calculating what corporate tax receipts in the early 1980s would have been if either the average tax rate or the profit rate had remained at its earlier level while the other changed over time. Actual corporate tax receipts averaged 49.6 billion 1986 dollars in 1981–1985. If the profitability of corporate assets had been the same as in the 1960s, tax receipts would have more than doubled to $110.4 billion. Even setting the profit rate equal to its value for 1976–1980 would have increased annual revenues by over $20 billion, to $72.5 billion. Fixing the average effective tax rate at its earlier level would also have raised taxes, though not by as much as the return to earlier profit levels. If the tax rate during the last five years had returned to its level in the early 1960s, taxes would have averaged $68.4 billion per year. Replacing the actual tax rate with its average value for the late 1970s would raise tax receipts by $13 billion to $62.5 billion per year.

2.2 INTERPRETING THE AVERAGE TAX RATE

Although our division of the tax-to-asset ratio into average tax rate and profit rate components may provide some insight into the source of declining tax revenues, the two components are not independent. The nature of the corporate income tax makes the average tax rate critically dependent upon the level of corporate profits. For taxable firms, many corporate tax deductions, such as depreciation allowances and tax credits, may be claimed regardless of the level of profits. A 1 percent increase in profits therefore raises the firm's taxable corporate income by more than 1 percent, increasing the average tax rate.

An offsetting effect arises for nontaxable firms. For firms with negative taxable income and no capacity to carry losses back against prior taxes, current tax payments will be zero regardless of how negative their real economic income is. An increase in profitability will not affect their taxes. It will, however, increase their economic profits, which enter the denominator of the average tax rate calculation for the entire corporate sector. These links between profitability and tax rates make it impossible to interpret changes in the average tax rate solely as the result of legislation.

A simple example can illustrate these points. Consider a firm that purchases a capital asset for $1,000 and is entitled to tax depreciation allowances of $150 per year, whereas the asset's true economic depreciation is $100 per year. If the firm uses no debt and has no other inputs to the production process, then its real economic profits are its receipts less $100. If the economic profit rate is 7 percent, receipts will equal $170 and the firm's taxable income will be $20. Assuming a flat-rate corporate income tax with a 0.50 marginal rate, the firm pays $10 in taxes for an average tax rate of $10/70 = 0.142$, and a tax-to-asset ratio of 0.01. Now consider what happens if the economic profit rate rises to 10 percent, bringing receipts to $200. Taxable income rises to $50, so taxes are $25, the tax-to-asset ratio is 0.025, and the average tax rate is 0.25. Shocks to corporate profits therefore affect measured average tax rates, even when the tax system is held constant.

To illustrate how, if some firms have tax losses, increased profits can lower the average tax rate, we introduce a second firm. It owns assets identical to those of the first firm, which earns a 7 percent return, but it operates in a different market with a 3 percent profit rate. Its receipts are $130, taxable income equals −$20, and it pays no taxes. The aggregate tax rate, computed by adding together the taxes of both firms and dividing by the sum of their profits, is 19.2 percent (25/130). The aggregate profit rate is 6.5 percent (130/2000). Now consider what happens if the second firm's profit rate rises to 5 percent. Its taxable income is now exactly zero, but it still pays no taxes, so the aggregate average tax rate is 16.7 percent (25/150), *down* from 19.2 percent. The aggregate profit rate rises to 7.5 percent, illustrating the possibility of a negative relationship between profitability and the aggregate average tax rate.

The sensitivity of average tax rates to economic conditions is only one of their many shortcomings as a measure of corporate tax burdens. It is well known (see Auerbach (1983) or Fullerton (1984)) that average tax rates may provide little information on the pattern of marginal tax incentives facing new investments. In addition, aggregate average tax rates may conceal important differences in tax burdens across different assets and different firms. Average corporate tax rates also provide an incomplete account of the tax burden on corporate income by ignoring the taxes paid by shareholders.

There are also measurement problems associated with average tax rates. They fail to consider "implicit taxes," such as the reduced returns received by banks that invest in municipal debt, as part of the total tax burden. Likewise, many sources of true economic income are ignored, since certain accounting practices that misstate economic income are not corrected. This problem even applies to the National Income Accounts.

An example of such a misstatement is the inappropriate timing of expenses under the completed contract accounting method. Accounting differences accentuate the problem of comparing average tax rates across industries.

3. Why Have Average Tax Rates Declined?

The last section demonstrated that declining profits and declining average tax rates are jointly responsible for the dramatic fall in corporate taxes. Despite numerous shortcomings, average tax rates do prove useful in analyzing changes in corporate tax revenues. They have also played an important part in the recent corporate tax reform debate. This section therefore extends our previous analysis by investigating the proximate causes of declining average tax rates. The source of recent changes in corporate profitability constitutes an unresolved puzzle, which is beyond the scope of this paper.[2]

3.1 STATUTORY TAX RATES VERSUS AVERAGE TAX RATES

Movements in average tax rates may be traced to changes in capital recovery provisions, the increased prevalence of firms with tax losses, increased use of investment tax credits, and other factors. Each of these factors causes the average tax rate to differ from the statutory maximum rate, as shown in Table 3. The first column in Table 3 shows the maximum statutory tax rate for each year from 1959 to 1985. The entries in the six middle columns describe how various factors have caused the average tax rate to differ from the statutory rate. Negative entries indicate factors that caused the average tax rate to be less than the statutory rate, and positive entries correspond to factors that increased the tax burden above the statutory rate. The average tax rate, Taxes/Profits, is reported in the last column. It is the sum of the maximum statutory tax rate plus the six adjustment factors in the middle columns. A detailed description of our methodology for decomposing the average tax rate is provided in the Appendix.

The first source of differences between statutory and average tax rates is increasingly generous capital recovery, as shown in the second column of Table 3. This term includes both the tax reduction from use of the investment tax credit, as well as that due to differences between tax depreciation and true economic depreciation. During the most recent five-

2. Since we are concerned primarily with the impact of legislative changes on tax receipts, we focus on the role of tax reforms in altering the average tax rate. Although tax changes may also affect revenues by altering profits, this effect is likely to be small over the time horizons we consider.

Table 3   CAUSES OF CHANGING AVERAGE TAX RATES, 1959–1985

Year	Statutory rate	Capital recovery	Other inflation effects	Tax losses	Foreign tax effects	Progres- sivity	Other factors	Average tax rate
1959	52.0	-3.1	-1.2	2.6	1.0	-3.4	1.7	49.7
1960	52.0	-4.2	-0.8	4.9	1.2	-3.4	1.5	51.1
1961	52.0	-4.4	-1.5	3.6	0.5	-3.8	1.7	48.0
1962	52.0	-9.5	-2.0	3.3	0.4	-3.6	1.4	42.1
1963	52.0	-9.3	-1.0	3.2	0.5	-3.5	1.7	43.5
1964	50.0	-9.2	-0.8	2.5	0.4	-3.7	1.3	40.5
1965	48.0	-8.6	-1.3	1.8	0.3	-3.2	1.1	38.2
1966	48.0	-8.5	-1.6	1.6	0.3	-3.2	1.0	37.7
1967	48.0	-9.5	-1.0	2.2	0.4	-3.3	1.3	38.0
1968	52.8	-9.6	-2.4	2.4	0.6	-3.9	1.0	40.9
1969	52.8	-10.0	-1.5	4.1	0.7	-4.2	1.5	43.4
1970	49.2	-9.7	-1.5	7.8	0.7	-3.2	2.1	45.4
1971	48.0	-8.5	-4.1	6.4	0.5	-2.9	2.1	41.5
1972	48.0	-10.5	-1.1	4.0	1.1	-2.9	2.0	40.6
1973	48.0	-11.1	1.5	3.1	1.8	-2.6	1.9	42.6
1974	48.0	-13.9	10.2	5.1	1.0	-2.1	1.9	50.2
1975	48.0	-8.0	-4.6	4.8	3.5	-2.9	1.7	42.4
1976	48.0	-7.9	0.9	3.6	-0.2	-2.6	1.6	43.4
1977	48.0	-8.3	-0.6	3.2	-1.2	-2.7	-0.3	38.2
1978	48.0	-8.5	0.3	3.0	-0.5	-3.1	-1.1	38.0
1979	46.0	-10.4	3.8	4.3	-0.9	-3.1	0.6	40.4
1980	46.0	-12.2	2.1	6.6	0.2	-3.3	1.3	40.6
1981	46.0	-17.3	-2.1	10.5	0.9	-2.5	0.9	36.4
1982	46.0	-26.3	-5.5	22.2	0.3	-3.8	1.2	34.2
1983	46.0	-21.8	-2.7	10.8	0.2	-3.7	2.9	31.7
1984	46.0	-21.2	-2.9	7.7	0.2	-3.7	2.1	28.2
1985	46.0	-24.2	-4.3	7.6	0.2	-3.7	1.9	23.6
Five-year averages								
1961–65	50.8	-8.2	-1.3	2.9	0.4	-3.5	1.4	42.5
1966–70	50.2	-9.5	-1.6	3.6	0.5	-3.6	1.5	41.1
1971–75	48.0	-9.5	0.4	4.7	1.6	-2.7	1.9	43.5
1976–80	47.2	-9.5	1.3	4.1	-0.5	-3.0	0.4	40.1
1981–85	46.0	-22.1	-3.5	11.8	0.4	-3.5	1.8	30.8

A detailed description of these calculations is presented in the Appendix. All entries for 1984 and 1985 are based on preliminary data and extrapolations. The average tax rate (column 8) equals the statutory rate (column 1) plus the adjustment factors in columns 2–7.

year period, capital recovery provisions accounted for a 22 percent differential between the statutory and the average tax rate. This is a substantial increase from the late 1970s, when these provisions explained a 9.5 percent difference between the two tax rates, or the 1960s, when these factors reduced the average tax rate by 8.9 percent.[3] Because generous capital recovery provisions have been one of the popular villains behind the recent decline in corporate taxes, we shall later provide a more detailed breakdown of these effects.

The third column in Table 3 reports the effect of inflation on average tax rates. This column combines two separate influences. First, inflation leads to spurious inventory profits that raise corporate tax payments and the average tax rate. (Inflation's positive impact through a related channel, the failure to index depreciation allowances for inflation, is subsumed in the capital recovery term above.) Inflation also exerts a countervailing effect on the average tax rate by reducing the real value of corporate debt, generating capital gains for equity holders. These gains are untaxed, so inflation raises economic income but does not affect taxes. The two effects roughly cancel, resulting in a small net effect of inflation on the average tax rate. Inflation raised the average tax rate by less than 1 percent during the 1970s, and it has reduced the average tax rate by 3.5 percent during the 1980s.

The fourth column in Table 3 indicates the impact of imperfect loss-offset provisions on the average tax rate. The principal effect of imperfect loss offset is to raise the average tax rate when firms experience losses, since firms with negative income cannot claim tax refunds. Tax receipts are therefore higher than they would be in a system with proportional taxation of economic income. This effect is somewhat attenuated by the availability of loss carrybacks and net operating loss carryforwards. Carrybacks allow some loss offset in the year when losses occur. Loss carryforwards, in contrast, reduce a firm's current tax liability as a result of previous losses.

Imperfect loss-offset provisions may raise or lower the average tax rate, depending on whether net operating loss deductions exceed the value of losses not carried back. The entries in column 4 of Table 3 show that throughout 1959 to 1985 imperfect loss offsets generated a substantial net increase in the average tax rate. For the most recent five years, the provisions regarding losses *increased* the average tax rate by 11.8 percent.

3. Our calculations may overstate the importance of capital recovery provisions in lowering the average tax rate, because we assume that all changes in the difference between tax and economic depreciation were actually claimed by firms. For firms carrying losses forward, this will overstate the importance of depreciation provisions and losses.

This is much larger than the impact of losses in any previous period. Imperfect loss offsets accounted for a 4.4 percent increase in the average tax rate in the 1970s and a 3.2 percent increase during the 1960s. This result deserves emphasis: the increased incidence of tax losses during the 1980s has increased, not reduced, the average corporate tax rate.

The fifth column of Table 3 describes how foreign tax provisions affect the average tax rate. This term consists of two parts. The first measures the increase in taxes that would have resulted if foreign source income were taxable at the U.S. statutory rate, and the second reduces taxes by the amount of foreign tax credits claimed. If the statutory tax rates in all other countries equaled that in the United States and all firms could utilize foreign tax credits in full, then the net foreign tax effect in our table would equal zero. If foreign countries levied taxes at rates below the domestic rate, the foreign tax effect would be positive since the domestic taxes on foreign source income would exceed the foreign tax credit. In our data, the net effect of foreign tax provisions is a small increase in the average tax rate. This effect averages 0.4 percent in the last five years.

The sixth and seventh columns of Table 3 indicate the influence of two other factors, tax progressivity and an "other" category, which includes posttabulation revisions and miscellaneous tax credits, on the average tax rate. Neither factor has a large effect. Tax progressivity, which accounts for the fact that some corporate income is taxed at rates below the statutory maximum, lowers the average tax rate by roughly 3.5 percent with little variation over time. The "other" category usually raises the average corporate tax rate, since the results of tax audits are included in this category and they outweigh the other tax credits.

Table 3 clearly suggests that the most important factor causing average tax rates to fall below the statutory rate is capital recovery. For the last five years, capital recovery provisions depressed the average tax rate by 14 percent more than they did during the 1960s and by 13 percent more than during the late 1970s. We now consider a more detailed breakdown of changes in capital recovery provisions.

3.2 CHANGES IN CAPITAL RECOVERY PROVISIONS

The capital recovery variable in Table 3 has two parts: one due to the capital consumption adjustment, and the other due to the investment tax credit. The capital consumption adjustment is the difference between tax depreciation and real economic depreciation. It has two components: accelerated depreciation and basis misstatement. Accelerated depreciation is the difference between tax depreciation and economic depreciation at historic cost. Tax depreciation is based on tax service lives and depreciation schedules. It usually provides larger depreciation allowances than would application of realistic economic lifetimes and decay patterns to the historic costs of corporate assets. Taxable income therefore understates economic income, reducing the average tax rate. The second term, basis misstatement, measures the difference between straight-line depreciation using economic asset lives but historic asset costs and that using the same decay profiles but revaluing assets each year to their current replacement cost. Failure to index the basis of depreciable assets raises taxable income above economic income and therefore increases the average tax rate.

The data in Table 4 show the relative importance of the three parts of the capital recovery aggregate. During the last five years, accelerated depreciation reduced the average tax rate by 35 percent, the investment tax credit (ITC) lowered it 13 percent, and inflationary misstatement of asset basis raised it by 26 percent. These large offsetting effects correspond to the net effect of -22 percent that is reported in the third column of Table 3. All three factors have become larger in absolute value during our sample period. In the 1960s, for example, accelerated depreciation lowered the average rate by 11.9 percent, inflation effects raised it by 5.4 percent, and the ITC lowered it by another 2.3 percent.

These results naturally raise the question of whether movements in the capital recovery factor are primarily the result of legislative changes, or whether they have been caused by other forces, such as a shift in the composition of investment toward equipment rather than structures. Although separating average tax rate movements into components due to legislative and other changes is a treacherous exercise, some illustrative calculations are nonetheless possible. Ziemer (1985) estimates the change in federal corporate tax revenues due to the passage of the Economic Recovery Tax Act of 1981 and the Tax Equity and Fiscal Responsibility Act of 1982, and presents a separate calculation for the impact of accelerated depreciation and other provisions. Using his revenue estimates, we calculate that the average tax rate would have been about 7 percent higher during the last four years if the accelerated cost and recovery system (ACRS) had not been adopted. This corresponds to increased revenues of $20 billion per year, on average, since 1982. The effect would have been largest in 1985, the year with the largest stock of assets receiving generous ACRS depreciation.

Although ACRS has lowered corporate taxes in the past four years, focusing only on the immediate postenactment effects of tax legislation can be misleading. Passage of a bill such as ERTA depresses corporate taxes by more in the period immediately after enactment than it does in

Table 4   BREAKDOWN OF CAPITAL RECOVERY COMPONENTS IN
AVERAGE TAX RATE

Year	Total effect	Accelerated depreciation	Inflation-induced misstatement of tax basis	Investment tax credit
			Percentage point change in average tax rate from	
1959	-3.1	-10.8	7.7	0.0
1960	-4.2	-12.6	8.3	0.0
1961	-4.4	-11.5	7.1	0.0
1962	-9.5	-12.7	5.7	-2.4
1963	-9.3	-12.2	5.0	-2.2
1964	-9.2	-11.1	4.2	-2.3
1965	-8.6	-9.5	3.5	-2.5
1966	-8.5	-9.3	3.5	-2.7
1967	-9.5	-10.9	4.3	-3.0
1968	-9.6	-11.6	5.1	-3.1
1969	-10.0	-13.5	6.2	-2.6
1970	-9.7	-17.0	8.8	-1.6
1971	-8.5	-14.5	8.5	-2.4
1972	-10.5	-15.0	8.5	-4.0
1973	-11.1	-14.8	8.1	-4.4
1974	-13.9	-21.6	13.4	-5.7
1975	-8.0	-17.6	17.3	-7.7
1976	-7.9	-15.2	16.0	-8.8
1977	-8.3	-14.4	14.2	-8.2
1978	-8.5	-14.7	14.6	-8.4
1979	-10.4	-17.6	17.2	-10.0
1980	-12.2	-22.6	21.7	-11.3
1981	-17.3	-30.0	26.8	-14.0
1982	-26.3	-50.2	43.3	-19.3
1983	-21.8	-36.9	26.3	-11.2
1984	-21.2	-29.0	17.1	-9.3
1985	-24.2	-28.6	15.0	-10.6
Five-year averages				
1961–1965	-8.2	-11.4	5.1	-1.9
1966–1970	-9.5	-12.5	5.6	-2.6
1971–1975	-10.4	-16.7	11.2	-4.9
1976–1980	-9.5	-16.9	16.7	-9.3
1981–1985	-22.1	-34.9	25.7	12.9

Data used to construct this table are drawn from the National Income Accounts, Table 8.7, and from the IRS *Statistics of Income Sourcebook*. Entries for 1984 and 1985 are based on preliminary or extrapolated data series. See the Appendix for further details.

the steady state. Immediately after enactment, revenues are reduced both because new assets are given substantial depreciation benefits immediately after installation, and because some relatively old pre-reform assets are still eligible for depreciation benefits under the previous, less generous depreciation rules. In the steady state, only the generous depreciation for new assets reduces revenues. This partially explains why, even without the TRA, corporate tax revenues were expected to rise during the late 1980s. An opposite effect arises with the recent legislation, which lengthens asset lives. It will collect more revenue in the short run than in the steady state, because some aging pre-TRA assets are paying higher taxes than they would have if they had been depreciated under the new rules.[4]

4. Corporate Taxes under the 1986 Tax Reform Act

The TRA shifts $120 billion of federal tax liability from households to corporations from 1987 to 1991. The TRA will therefore affect both the average tax rate and the tax-to-asset ratio for nonfinancial corporations. This section uses revenue projections from the Congressional Budget Office (CBO) (1986) to estimate the course of average tax rates over the next five years. It compares the tax trajectory without the TRA with the trajectory under the new legislation, and places the increased corporate tax burden in historical perspective.

Table 5 compares the paths of corporate tax payments under old law and the TRA. A detailed description of the calculations is provided in the Appendix. The first panel shows the level of corporate tax payments by NFCs in 1986 dollars under the two regimes. Even under old law, corporate taxes are projected to rise. By 1990, for example, they will be 77 percent higher than in the first five years of the 1980s. Rising corporate tax payments can be traced to two sources. First, corporate profits are forecast to rise in the late 1980s. Our CBO-based projections imply a profit rate of 8.2 percent during 1987–1991, compared with 4.9 percent in the early 1980s. In addition, the front-loading of depreciation under ACRS implies that the average tax rate on projects undertaken since 1981 is low early in the project's life and high later on. As more projects reach the high-tax stage of their life cycle, corporate taxes also rise.

Under the TRA, revenues rise even more rapidly than under old law.

---

4. Although revenues will be lower immediately after a tax reform like ERTA than they will be in the steady state, it does not follow that tax revenues two years after the reform are higher than those in the year after the reform. There is a countervailing revenue-reducing effect: as the stock of assets being depreciated under the generous new rules rises, tax receipts may decline.

By 1990, corporate taxes from the NFCs will exceed $100 billion (1986 dollars), more than double the level of the past five years. For 1987 to 1991, corporate taxes are 22 percent greater under the TRA than under current law. The new bill's revenue impact is largest in 1987, when it raises over 30 percent more revenue than the current law. The reason is that rates remain high, but most tax preferences have been eliminated.

The two lower panels of Table 5 show corporate taxes relative to GNP and corporate assets. Under current law the tax-to-GNP ratio would rise from 1.2 percent in 1985 to 1.8 percent in 1991 while the TRA raises this ratio to 2.2 percent. The new law therefore returns the tax-to-GNP ratio to its level during the late 1970s but not to the level (3.2 percent on average) of the 1960s. A similar statement applies to the ratio of tax payments to net NFC assets, which is plotted in Figure 1. From an average of 1.5 percent during 1981 to 1985, this tax measure rises to 2.6 percent under old law and to 3.1 percent under new law by 1991. The new law will

Table 5   PROJECTED CORPORATE TAX REVENUES, 1986–1991

| Year | NFC federal tax payments ($1986 billion) | |
	Old law	New law
1986	56.0	61.5
1987	69.9	90.9
1988	79.2	96.9
1989	83.6	99.4
1990	87.7	103.6
1991	90.3	107.8
Year	NFC federal taxes as percent of GNP	
	Old law	New law
1986	1.3	1.5
1987	1.6	2.1
1988	1.8	2.2
1989	1.8	2.1
1990	1.8	2.2
1991	1.8	2.2
Year	NFC federal taxes as percent of net NFC assets	
	Old law	New law
1986	1.7	1.9
1987	2.1	2.7
1988	2.3	2.9
1989	2.4	2.9
1990	2.5	3.0
1991	2.6	3.1

Data entries correspond to calendar years and were constructed using Congressional Budget Office (1986) forecasts of corporate taxes and GNP under the old law, augmented by Joint Tax Committee estimates of the revenue effects of the Tax Reform Act of 1986.

double the ratio of taxes to corporate assets, although this ratio will still be lower than it was during the 1960s.

Although part of the change in tax revenues is due to anticipated increases in corporate profits, the average tax rate will also change significantly during the next five years. This change is shown in the first two rows of Table 6, which report the average tax rates under old law and under the TRA for 1986 to 1991. Without any legislative change, the average tax rate would have increased from 0.24 in 1985 to 0.30 by 1990. This is higher than in the first five years of the 1980s but still below the level of the late 1970s. Under new law, by comparison, the average tax rate rises to 0.36 by the end of the decade, almost returning to its level of the late 1970s. The TRA has its largest impact on the tax rate in the transition period, 1987 and 1988, when the ratio of taxes to economic profits rises by 8.1 percent and 6.5 percent, respectively. Figure 2 plots the movements in average tax rates for 1959 to 1985 as well as for the next five years under both old and new laws.

The TRA changes numerous provisions in the corporate income tax. The Joint Tax Committee's revenue estimates, for example, include seven-

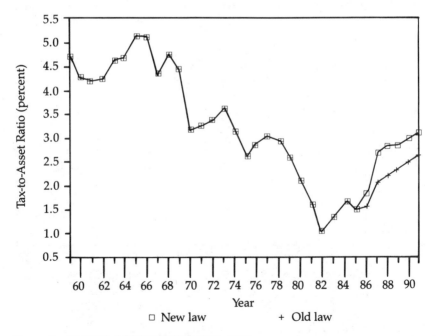

Figure 1   TAX-TO-ASSET RATIO, 1959–1991

Table 6   PROJECTED AVERAGE TAX RATES, 1986–1991

	Year					
	1986	1987	1988	1989	1990	1991
Average tax rate (old law)	22.9	26.8	29.0	29.7	30.2	29.9
Average tax rate (new law)	25.1	34.9	35.5	35.3	35.7	35.7
Tax rate differential new law—old law	2.2	8.1	6.5	5.6	5.5	5.8
Differential due to						
statutory rate	0.0	-6.0	-12.0	-12.0	-12.0	-12.0
capital recovery	1.5	5.6	6.5	8.4	9.6	11.0
accounting rules	1.0	4.1	4.9	4.3	3.5	2.4
other factors	-0.3	4.4	7.1	4.9	4.4	4.4

Calculations are based on Congressional Budget Office (1986) projections of corporate profits and tax revenues under pre-1986 law, combined with Joint Tax Committee forecasts of revenue changes from the Tax Reform Act of 1986.

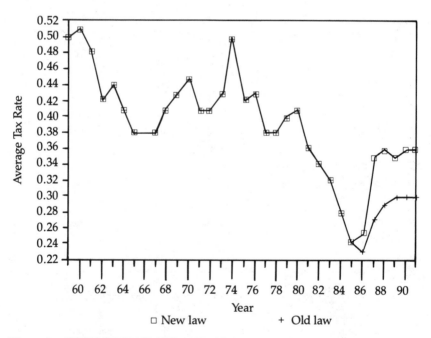

Figure 2   AVERAGE TAX RATE, 1959–1991

teen major categories and hundreds of minor categories through which revenue changes occur. A detailed analysis of why the average tax rate will differ from the statutory rate is impossible because many of the required data series are unavailable. We can, however, provide a rough sketch of why the average tax rate changes under the new law.

The last four rows in Table 6 disaggregate changes in the effective tax rate between old law and the TRA into four categories. The first, the change in the statutory rate, reduces the average rate. There are no rate changes for 1986. In 1987, the statutory rate falls by 6 percent to the 40 percent "blended" rate for a company whose fiscal year coincides with the calendar year. Beginning in calendar 1988, the top statutory rate is 34 percent.

Several provisions offset the statutory rate reduction and raise the average tax rate. The next row shows the impact of changes in capital recovery provisions, principally the repeal of the ITC and the extension of tax depreciation lives. This accounts for an 11 percent increase in the average tax rate in 1991. In the earlier years, it is somewhat less important, principally because transition rules allow a substantial share of the investment undertaken prior to 1988 to obtain favorable tax treatment.[5]

The penultimate row in Table 6 shows how changes in accounting rules affect the average tax rate. There are important provisions in this category, including changes affecting long-term contracts, the capitalization of construction and development costs, and the treatment of capital gains on installment obligations. These accounting changes raise the average tax rate by nearly 5 percent in 1988, and by an average of 3.8 percent during 1987 to 1991.[6] The final row of Table 6 shows how various other factors cause the average tax rate under the new law to differ from

5. Our measure of the average tax rate change due to capital recovery may understate the actual impact of the new law because of the interaction between depreciation provisions and the strengthened minimum tax. For firms with substantial depreciation deductions, the new minimum tax may raise tax payments. This is classified as an effect of the minimum tax, not depreciation rules, in our analysis.

6. An important caveat applies to the accounting-induced change in average tax rates. Table 6 reports the accounting-induced change in taxes divided by our measure of economic income. Each accounting change, however, also affects the measured value of economic income. Repeal of the completed contract method of accounting, for example, will change the IRS measure of receipts less deductions that forms the basis for our profits variable. Average tax rates computed relative to measured economic income under the new tax regime, therefore, would be slightly lower than those reported here, because income will be higher as a result of these accounting changes. Average tax rates in all previous years, computed relative to an economic income measure that did not allow for deferred accrual under the completed contract method, would be lower than those reported in Tables 2 and 3. The change in average rates over time is not affected by the choice of convention for economic income, even though the level of the average rate is.

that under previous law. These provisions include the strengthened minimum tax, changes in foreign tax credit provisions, and revenues from increased tax compliance. These miscellaneous provisions increase the average tax rate by 4.4 percent in 1991.

Although our calculations of the factors behind changes in average tax rates are necessarily uncertain, they do underscore two important features of the TRA. First, changes in capital recovery provisions will significantly raise corporate taxes. By the late 1980s, the differential between the statutory and the average tax rate that will be attributable to capital recovery rules will return to its level in the 1960s and 1970s. The TRA therefore reverses the changes of the early 1980s, when the combination of accelerated depreciation and investment credits lowered average tax rates by as much as 25 percent. Second, many of the important revenue-raising provisions in the new law are excluded from the usual economic analysis of corporate tax incentives. Marginal effective tax rate calculations, such as those in King and Fullerton (1984), do not usually incorporate particular accounting rules, minimum taxes, or many of the other provisions that have an important effect on corporate investment incentives.

5. Conclusions

This paper explores why corporate tax revenues have declined for the last thirty years. Contrary to many claims, legislative changes explain less than half of the decline in revenues since the mid-1960s. The decline in corporate profits, which averaged nearly 11 percent of the value of net corporate assets during the 1960s, as compared with just under 5 percent in the 1980s, is a more important factor.

Declining corporate tax revenues have been accompanied by a decline in the average tax rate, the ratio of corporate taxes to economic profits. Although this average tax rate is of limited value for analyzing the incentive effects of the corporate tax, it has attracted widespread attention in the recent tax reform discussion. Changes in both the tax law and the rate of corporate profits affect the average tax rate. The change in depreciation provisions between the late 1970s and the early 1980s reduced the average tax rate by roughly 13 percent.

The TRA, which raises $120 billion in corporate taxes over the next five years, accelerates the trend toward rising average tax rates that would have occurred under old law. Reduced capital recovery allowances and other changes in the 1986 Act will combine to raise average effective tax rates to 36 percent by 1990, compared with 31 percent in the first five years of the 1980s. Corporate taxes as a share of GNP and relative to corporate assets will also rise significantly. By 1990, federal tax payments will equal 3 percent of net corporate assets, well above their level in the early 1980s and approximately equal to their asset share in the late 1970s. Taxes will still remain a smaller fraction of assets than they were in the 1960s, however, in part because corporate profitability is projected to be well below its level two decades ago. Although we focus on the TRA's revenue impact over the next five years, this is a potentially misleading indicator of a tax bill's revenue effects. By lengthening the depreciation lives of many assets, the new law raises corporate tax revenues in the short run at the expense of some reduction in future years. The inherent uncertainty in long-range forecasts, however, makes it difficult to quantify these effects.

Much of our analysis implicitly divorces the average tax rate from the corporate profit rate, although such a separation is impossible. Because corporate taxes do not rise proportionally with corporate profits, changes in the profit rate have a direct influence on the average tax rate. Over longer horizons, the average tax rate may also affect the profit rate, at least if average and marginal tax rates move in tandem. Higher tax burdens will induce offsetting reductions in capital investment, which should increase pretax profitability.

Finally, our analysis of revenue changes in the TRA suggests that a wide range of corporate tax provisions that have important revenue effects are typically ignored in the economic analysis of the corporate income tax. These provisions affect the average and marginal tax rates on new investment and deserve to be incorporated in future work.

TECHNICAL APPENDIX
DESCRIPTION OF THE AVERAGE TAX RATE DECOMPOSITION
AND DATA SOURCES

This Appendix explains how we allocate changes in the average tax rate into various components, describes our measures of tax payments and economic income for nonfinancial corporations, and presents a detailed account of our post-1986 projections.

The Average Tax Rate Decomposition Our average tax rate decomposition begins from the definition of federal tax receipts from the NFCs:

$$\text{Taxes} = \tau\lambda\text{ISTT} - \text{Cbacks} - \text{ITC} - \text{FTC} - \text{Othcred} + \text{Retab.} \quad (A1)$$

ISTT denotes income subject to tax, τ is the maximum statutory corporate tax rate, and λ is a "progressivity parameter" reflecting the fact that not all taxable income is taxed at the top marginal rate. All the terms on the right side of (A1) are directly available, except for λ. We estimate λ, using data from the *Statistics of income sourcebook*, as $\lambda =$ Taxbefcred$/\tau$ISTT, where Taxbefcred is taxes payable before computation of credits. Investment tax credits (ITC), foreign tax credits (FTC), other credits (Othcred), and loss carrybacks (Cbacks) reduce corporate tax receipts. Retab, which corresponds to the results of Internal Revenue Service (IRS) audits and other changes in previous returns, is typically positive and therefore raises revenue. Note that our measures of tax credits correspond to actual, not potential, credits; limits on the use of tax credits may induce substantial differences between the two in recent years (see Altshuler and Auerbach (1986) for a discussion).

Whereas taxes are levied on income subject to tax, average tax rates are calculated relative to the real economic income of shareholders, denoted by Profits. Income subject to tax and economic income are related by the identity

$$\text{Profits} = \text{ISTT} + \text{NTI} + \text{NOL} + \text{CCADJ} + \text{IVA} + \text{Debtgain} - \text{FSI}, \quad \text{(A2)}$$

where NTI is the net income of firms with current losses and zero taxable income, NOL is the statutory deduction for net operating losses incurred in previous years, CCADJ is the National Income Accounts capital consumption adjustment (the difference between tax and economic depreciation), IVA is the inventory valuation adjustment (again from NIPA) that measures the spurious profits that result from inflation on goods in inventory, Debtgain is the transfer from bondholders to equity holders that takes place when inflation reduces the value of outstanding debt, and FSI is the foreign source income of U.S. corporations. A very helpful reference for understanding the relationship between IRS and National Income Accounts measures of corporate profits is the U.S. Department of Commerce (1985).

Equations (A1) and (A2) can be combined to obtain an expression for tax receipts in terms of economic income. Dividing through this expression by economic income yields

$$\text{Taxes/Profits} = \tau\lambda - \tau\lambda(\text{NTI} + \text{NOL} + \text{CCADJ} + \text{IVA} + \text{Debtgain} - \text{FSI})/\text{Profits} - (\text{ITC} + \text{FTC} + \text{Othcred})/\text{Profits} + \text{Cbacks/Profits} + \text{Retab/Profits}. \quad \text{(A3)}$$

We rewrite this expression by grouping together related terms:

$$
\begin{aligned}
\text{Taxes/Profits} = {} & \tau - \tau\lambda(\text{CCADJ} + \text{ITC})/\text{Profits} - \tau\lambda(\text{IVA} \\
& + \text{Debtgain})/\text{Profits} - \tau\lambda(\text{NOL} + \text{NTI})/\text{Profits} \\
& + \text{Cbacks/Profits} - (\text{FTC} - \tau\lambda\text{FSI})/\text{Profits} + \tau(\lambda - 1) \\
& - \text{Othcred} + \text{Retab/Profits.} \quad \text{(A4)}
\end{aligned}
$$

The first term on the right side of (A4) is the maximum statutory tax rate. The six adjustments to the statutory rate required to obtain the average tax rate correspond to the entries in Table 3.

The first adjustment involves capital recovery provisions. It is the sum of ITCs and CCADJ, the difference between tax depreciation and economic depreciation of corporate assets at replacement cost. The National Income Accounts also disaggregate the CCADJ into the components due to accelerated depreciation at historic cost and inflationary misstatement of basis; this breakdown is used in Table 4.

The next adjustment term corresponds to the other distortions of profits related to inflation. It includes the inventory valuation adjustment and the inflation-induced gain on corporate debt. National Income and Product Accounts (NIPA) convention defines IVA as a negative quantity; the average tax rate is therefore increasing in the IVA, which in turn is an increasing function of inflation. Debtgain is positive, however, and reduces the average tax rate during periods of high inflation, because the inflation-induced gains of the equity holders are not part of the tax base, so they yield income but no tax liability. The net effect of these two factors depends upon the level of leverage and the stock of inventories held in the corporate sector.

The third adjustment term concerns corporate losses and consists of three parts. The first is the net income of firms with zero taxable income, the second adds net operating loss deductions back into taxable income, and the third adjusts for the use of current losses to obtain carryback refunds. Again there are countervailing effects. Higher levels of both NOL deductions and carryback refunds reduce the average corporate tax rate relative to what it would be in a system that taxed current economic income. Increases in the losses accruing to currently nontaxable firms, however, raise the average tax rate. (NTI is a negative number, so an "increase in losses" is a reduction of NTI, although an increase in its absolute value.) Losses raise the average tax rate because economic income is computed by netting the income of firms with positive profits against the income of firms with losses. For tax purposes, however, this offset does not take place. Firms with positive profits pay taxes, and those with negative earnings receive nothing. Imperfect loss-offset provisions therefore cause losses to raise the average tax rate.

The fourth adjustment to the statutory rate involves foreign income and tax credits. The adjustment term equals the tax liability that would have been due on foreign source income if it had been earned in the United States, minus foreign tax credits claimed. Since foreign tax credits are subject to a variety of limitations, the net effect of these two factors is usually to raise average tax rates. Our treatment of foreign source income also induces a potential relationship between foreign tax rates and the measured average tax rate on domestic income. For example, income earned in a country with a corporate tax rate below λ_T will face additional tax when repatriated to a U.S. firm. This will raise our measured average tax rate on domestic income. Such effects are inevitable in any calculation such as ours that considers the domestic tax rate in one nation rather than the worldwide tax rate on worldwide income.

The two remaining adjustments are straightforward. The fifth, for the progressivity of the tax code, measures the change in the average tax rate due to taxing some positive-income firms at rates below the statutory maximum. It always reduces the average tax rate, since about 10 percent of the positive taxable income accruing to corporations is taxed at rates below the statutory maximum. The final term combines other tax credits with retabulations. Other tax credits are important primarily in recent years, when they include the R&D Tax Credit, the New Jobs Credit, and various energy-related credits. Retabulations consist primarily of audit profits and minor adjustments to tax returns filed in previous years.

Data Sources Most of the data series used in our analysis are drawn from either the National Income and Product Accounts (NIPA), supplemented by unpublished NIPA data, or the IRS *Corporation sourcebook of statistics of income*. In some cases, the data series for 1984 and 1985 are based on preliminary data or have been constructed by extrapolating 1983 values.

The NIPAs present data on federal corporate profits tax liability for the entire corporate sector, but not for the NFCs. (NIPA also presents total tax liabilities to all governments, divided into financial and nonfinancial sectors.) We construct our own estimate of NFC federal taxes, following the NIPA approach for all corporations as in NIPA Table 8.13. Our tax measure is

Taxes = Income Taxes Before Credits (SOI) − Tax Credits (SOI)
　　　　 − Carryback Refunds (NIPA) + Other Retabulations
　　　　 (NIPA)　(A5)

The first two variables are drawn from *Statistics of income* for 1959 to 1983. Our sample period begins in 1959 because that is when the IRS began publishing information on Income Subject to Tax, one of the variables used in constructing corporate profits. We construct a measure for the nonfinancial corporate sector as All Returns − Finance Insurance and Real Estate + Insurance Agents + Real Estate Operators. This is not exactly coincident with the NIPA definition, which also includes some holding companies that cannot be separately identified from the SOI data, but the differences between the two series are trivial. Carrybacks and other retabulations are drawn from unpublished data used to construct NIPA Table 8.13. Our data on these series are for the entire corporate sector, because a breakdown for financial versus nonfinancial firms is not available. The errors associated with the inclusion of financial firms in these aggregates are also likely to be small.

For 1984 and 1985, our measures of tax credits are based on forecasts provided by the Joint Tax Committee. We extrapolated Income Taxes Before Credits by extrapolating total taxes, using NIPA data on NFC tax liability to all levels of government, and then adjusting it for the credit terms on the right side. We obtained data on the sum of carrybacks and retabulations from the preliminary NIPAs, and assumed carrybacks remained constant at their 1983 level to divide the series into its two components.

We define real economic profits of the nonfinancial corporate sector as

$$
\begin{aligned}
\text{Profits} = \ & \text{Income Subject to Tax (SOI)} + \text{Net Operating Loss} \\
& \text{Deductions (SOI)} + \text{Negative Taxable Income (SOI)} \\
& + \text{CCADJ (NIPA)} + \text{IVA (NIPA)} + \text{Debtgain} - \text{FSI} \quad \text{(A6)}
\end{aligned}
$$

The data series for Income Subject to Tax and NOL deductions are drawn from *Statistics of income*. IVA is reported in the NIPA in Table 1.16. The measurements of NTI, CCADJ, Debtgain, and FSI require discussion.

NTI is the net income of firms with zero taxable income. It is computed as the difference between the entries for net income in the *Sourcebook* tables for (i) firms with and without net income, and (ii) firms with net income. NTI is this difference minus the net income differential for Subchapter S corporations and the special statutory deductions for firms with no taxable income.

Although a measure of CCADJ is reported in the National Income Accounts, we amend it slightly for our analysis. We augment the NIPA measure of CCADJ (Table 8.4) with the depletion adjustment for domestic minerals and the adjustment to depreciate expenditures for oil shafts, wells, and exploration from NIPA Table 8.12. These are additional cases in which tax depreciation differs from economic depreciation, so these terms must be added to the accelerated depreciation component of CCADJ.

Debtgain is defined as the fourth-quarter-to-fourth-quarter percentage change in the GNP deflator times the market value of outstanding NFC debt at the end of the previous year. The time series for debt at market value is described in Feldstein and Jun (1986).

FSI is measured as foreign service taxable income minus loss (before recapture), as reported in various issues of the *Statistics of Income Bulletin*. This corresponds to current taxable income from foreign sources. Unfortunately, this data series is not available for every year since 1959; it is available for fourteen of the years between 1961 and 1982. We interpolated and extrapolated these data to other years when necessary.

Our measure of economic profits differs from that in the National Income Accounts in several ways. The most important is its inclusion of the equity holders' capital gain on corporate debt during inflationary periods. In addition, the National Income Accounts include net foreign source equity income of all U.S. residents in the measured corporate profits. We also include the 15 percent of intercorporate dividends not exempt from taxation, because the data required to remove this component of IRS taxable income were not available before 1978.

All of the series based on NIPA data were available through 1985 except for the depletion and oil exploration adjustments, which were available through 1983. We constructed 1984 and 1985 values for these series as well as the NOL and NTI series from the IRS by assuming they remained constant at their real 1983 levels. We assumed λ remained constant at its 1983 value, and updated ISTT as ISTT = Taxbefcred/$\tau\lambda$, using our Taxbefcred forecast.

Finally, we measured the current replacement cost of the net tangible assets held in the nonfinancial corporate sector, using the Federal Reserve Board's *Balance sheets of the U.S. economy*. The *Balance sheets* report year-end values, which we averaged to construct the midyear value for the denominator of our profit rate calculations. We subtract the Feldstein–Jun (1986) measure of the market value of corporate debt to obtain a series for the net assets of the corporate sector.

Revenue and Average Tax Rate Projections, 1986–1991 Most of our calculations for 1986 to 1991 rely on data from the Congressional Budget Office (1986). We use their GNP projections and inflation forecasts for the GNP deflator throughout our calculation.

Our profit variable, Profits, has two components. One corresponds loosely to real economic profits in the NIPA; the other is Debtgain. To calculate the Profits components other than Debtgain, we use the CBO forecast of real corporate profits on an NIPA basis, ProfitsNIPA. We compute the ratio (Profits − Debtgain)/ProfitsNIPA for 1984 and 1985; the ratios are 0.747 and 0.703, respectively. Using an average ratio of 0.725, we forecast Profits − Debtgain based on the CBO forecasts and then add in Debtgain, calculated as the CBO inflation rate times our extrapolation of corporate debt (which is the 1985 value extrapolated at the nominal GNP growth rate).

We compute NFC tax liabilities under old law, using the CBO's forecasts of fiscal year corporate tax receipts (p. 63) minus projected receipts from Federal Reserve banks (taken from the OMB federal budget projections for fiscal year (FY) 1987 and years through 1989, with extrapolation through 1991, holding the series constant in real terms). This tax measure is a fiscal year indicator of accruals from the whole corporate sector. We use the ratio of NFC to total federal taxes in 1985 (0.885) to scale this profit measure for the NFCs, and then convert to calendar years by averaging adjacent fiscal years with weights of 0.75 and 0.25, respectively. When projections for FY 1992 were needed, we assumed that the fiscal 1991 value grew at the same rate as between FY 1990 and 1991.

Total federal revenues for fiscal years through 1991 are reported in the CBO (p. 63). We calculated calendar year revenues as a weighted average, and found the calendar 1991 value by increasing the calendar 1990 value in the same proportion as the fiscal 1991 revenue forecast relative to the fiscal 1990 forecast. We extrapolated the net replacement value of NFC assets, assuming they grew in real terms at 1.64 percent per year, the average growth rate for 1980 through 1985, and fully reflected inflation in the GNP deflator.

Finally, to measure the revenue changes associated with the 1986 TRA, we rely upon the Joint Tax Committee's revenue estimates presented in House of Representatives (1986). We estimate the total tax effect for nonfinancial corporations as the total change in corporate revenues minus the changes due to taxation of insurance companies and financial institutions (titles IX and X of the revenue estimates) minus 0.115 times the revenue changes for the minimum tax, pension provisions, compliance, and miscellaneous other provisions (titles VII, XI, XV, and XVII). This correction adjusts for the share of these revenue changes that arise from the financial corporations. We adjust all revenue estimates from fiscal to calendar years using weighted averages, and construct fiscal 1992 estimates by assuming the fiscal 1991 value grows at the same rate as it did between fiscal 1990 and fiscal 1991. Our measure of capital recovery changes is just the revenue change due to title II, capital cost provisions, and that for accounting reforms is the revenue estimate in title VIII.

REFERENCES

Altshuler, Rosanne, and Alan J. Auerbach. 1986. The significance of tax law asymmetries: An empirical investigation. University of Pennsylvania, Department of Economics. Mimeo.

Auerbach, Alan J. 1983. Corporate taxation in the United States. *Brookings Papers on Economic Activity* 2: 451–513.

Board of Governors of the Federal Reserve System. 1986. *Balance sheets of the U.S. economy.* Washington, D.C.: Board of Governors.

Congressional Budget Office. 1985. *Revising the corporate income tax.* Washington, D.C.: U.S. Government Printing Office.

———. 1986. *The economic and budget outlook: An update.* Washington, D.C.: U.S. Government Printing Office.

Feldstein, Martin S., Louis Dicks-Mireaux, and James Poterba. 1983. The effective tax rate and the pretax rate of return. *Journal of Public Economics* 21: 129–58.

Feldstein, Martin S., and Joosung Jun. 1986. The market value of corporate debt and the changing debt-capital ratio. Forthcoming.

Feldstein, Martin S., and Lawrence H. Summers. 1979. Inflation and the taxation of capital in the corporate sector. *National Tax Journal* 32: 445–70.

Fullerton, Don. 1984. Which effective tax rate? *National Tax Journal* 37: 23–41.

Joint Committee on Taxation. 1984. *Study of 1983 effective tax rates of selected large U.S. corporations.* Washington, D.C.: U.S. Government Printing Office.

King, Mervyn A., and Don Fullerton. 1984. *The taxation of income from capital.* Chicago: University of Chicago Press.

McIntyre, Robert S. 1984. *Corporate income taxes in the Reagan years: A study of three years of legalized tax avoidance.* Washington, D.C.: Citizens for Tax Justice.

Neubig, Thomas, and C. Eugene Steuerle. 1983. The taxation of income flowing through financial institutions: General framework and a summary of tax issues. Office of Tax Analysis, U.S. Treasury Department Working Paper no. 52.

Spooner, Gillian. 1986. Effective tax rates from financial statements. *National Tax Journal* 39: 293–306.

U.S. Department of Commerce, Bureau of Economic Analysis. 1985. Corporate profits before tax, profits liability, and dividends. BEA Methodology Paper MP-2. Washington, D.C.: U.S. Government Printing Office.

U.S. Department of the Treasury. 1985. Internal Revenue Service. *Statistics of income: Corporation income tax returns, 1982.* Washington, D.C.: U.S. Government Printing Office.

U.S. House of Representatives. 1986. Tax Reform Act of 1986: Conference report to accompany H.R. 3838. Report 99-841. Washington, D.C.: U.S. Government Printing Office.

Ziemer, Richard C. 1985. Impact of recent tax law changes. *Survey of Current Business* 65 (April): 28–31.

John B. Shoven

Stanford University and NBER

The Tax Consequences of Share Repurchases and Other Non-Dividend Cash Payments to Equity Owners

You know something is happening, but you don't know what it is, do you Mr. Jones.

"Ballad of a Thin Man," Bob Dylan

The financial behavior of corporations has changed greatly in the last ten years. Previously, most of the cash that stockholders received from corporations took the form of dividends, and the dividend cash flow was the ultimate determinant of the value of equities. Recently, as this paper will document, dividends have been surpassed by nondividend cash distributions to shareholders. These distributions are the sum of share repurchases and cash mergers. In 1985, more than half of the money received by shareholders from corporations was for the acquisition of shares.

The growth of nondividend cash payments to shareholders has major consequences for our understanding of share valuation and investment as well as for revenue projections of the U.S. Treasury. In particular, the fact that the financial behavior of companies has changed so significantly (and without much recognition) calls into question the forecasts that the new tax law will increase corporate tax collections by $120 billion. To pre-

Preliminary draft of a paper to be presented at the Economics of Tax Policy conference of the NBER to be held in Washington, D.C. on November 17, 1986. It is not for quotation without permission. This work was made possible by the tireless work and intellectual stimuli provided by Laurie B. Simon, who is also doing research on this subject. It also benefited greatly from the research assistance of Karen Prindle and Karen Van Nuys. Larry Summers and Jim Poterba gave me extremely useful advice.

dict tax collections in a new tax environment, one has to understand the behavior of firms. In terms of payments to stockholders, the times are changing.

Dividends have been central to economists' models of the valuation of corporate equity. The value of a share of a corporation's stock is taken to be the present discounted value of future cash payments to be received by the owners of that share, where those cash payments are taken to be dividends. Further, the value of equity is important to the economy. One leading model of corporate investment has investment depending crucially on the financial valuation of the firm (see, for example, Tobin (1969) or Summers (1981)). Thus, we have dividends being the fundamental determinant of share value, and share value being an important factor in the strength of investment.

There are problems, however, with pursuing this line of reasoning. Certainly, the financial valuation of the firm is the present value of the properly discounted stream of cash payments returned to investors. The first problem with the model driven by dividends is that a large fraction of the cash payments to stockholders does not take the form of dividends, as this paper will document. Presumably, these other cash payments are determinants of the value of corporate equity. The second problem is that, as a profession, we do not have a very good explanation for the payment of dividends in the first place. Under the current tax code, dividends are a distinctly tax-disadvantaged way to transmit cash between the firm and its investors relative to other available financial strategies. Their existence presumably indicates either that dividends convey a valuable signal to stockholders about the management's perception of future earnings prospects (Miller and Rock (1984)) or that the payment of dividends restricts the actions of management in a manner that helps reduce the control problems brought about by the separation of management and ownership (Jensen and Meckling (1976)). Whether these explanations are adequate to account for the actual level of dividends, given their tax handicap, has continued to be debated.

The tax problem with equity financing in general, and dividend paying equity in particular, is that two levels of taxation must be paid on the incremental earnings resulting from investments financed by these means. First, the corporation income tax applies with a federal marginal tax rate of 46 percent. Second, the remaining 54 percent of earnings are subject to the personal income tax if the investor is a household and if the funds are paid out as a dividend. Even if the money is retained at the corporate level, it will be implicitly taxed; the market will capitalize the fact that eventually it will be subject to personal dividend taxation when it is remitted to shareholders. Thus, an after corporate tax dollar in the corporate treasury will be valued at less than a dollar. If dividends are the only means of returning cash to investors, an after corporate tax dollar will be valued at the ratio of one minus the marginal personal tax rate of shareholders to one minus the effective marginal tax rate on accrued capital gains. However, the assumption that dividends are the only way to return cash to a firm's financiers is incorrect.

An alternative strategy, of course, is to use debt finance. Its advantage is that interest payments are deductible from the corporation income tax, and thus the return to debtholders is subject to only personal taxation. Most models of optimal corporate financial structure involve the firm trading off the tax advantages of debt against its inflexibility and hence the increased chance of incurring the costs associated with bankruptcy.[1] The taxation of debt at the personal level may be reduced by the use of pension funds and other retirement accumulation tax shelters.

Even for equity, there are ways other than dividends to return cash to stockholders that involve far lower total taxes and, therefore, more value to investors. One such method is the repurchase of shares by the company. In the absence of information, problems between stockholders and management, and in the absence of taxes and transaction costs, dividends and share repurchase programs are equivalent. If a company uses the same amount of money to buy back shares or pay dividends, the total value of the firm will be the same after either transaction. It will have the same debt-equity ratio, the same real assets, the same opportunities, and therefore the same value. In the share repurchase case, each shareholder can sell sufficient shares to match the cash flow he would have received in the dividend case. In the dividend case, dividend recipients can use the proceeds to buy additional shares in the company and therefore match the percentage interest they would have had if they had been among the stockholders who did not sell in a share repurchase program.

Taxes cause a major break in this equivalence to the disadvantage of dividends and, therefore, to the relative advantage of share repurchase. It is still true that the total equity value of the firm should be the same after the payment of an equivalent amount of cash in either dividend or

1. While under the assumptions of Modigliani and Miller (1958) (in the world without taxes and bankruptcy costs), "the market value of one firm is independent of its capital structure" (p. 268), the optimal capital structure becomes 100 percent debt with the incorporation of corporate taxes (Modigliani and Miller (1963)). However, there exists voluminous literature on the effect of bankruptcy costs limiting the use of this tax-advantaged debt. See, for example, Stiglitz (1972), Kraus and Litzenberger (1973), Kim (1978), Modigliani (1982), and Gordon (1982), where it is argued "that the tax advantage to using debt is in equilibrium just offset at the margin by the additional agency costs and possible bankruptcy costs incurred as a result of the extra debt" (Gordon 1982, p. 462).

share repurchase form. This equivalence rests on the idea that the firm has the same assets, capital structure, and future opportunities in either case. If the cash was paid out as a dividend, then it is fully taxable with the exception of the modest $100 exclusion offered under current law. However, if it was paid out as a repurchase, the payment results in a capital gain to shareholders of the amount of the purchase. However, most of this capital gain is accrued and not realized.

To make the share repurchase strategy absolutely clear, consider the simple example outlined in Table 1. A company is originally financed by the issue of 100 shares at $10 each. The company uses the $1000 proceeds to purchase productive capital, and after a year it has realized a $100 profit. The competitive market value of the firm is now $1100 ($11 per share) because the company now consists of a fully restored $1000 machine and $100 cash.

Consider two strategies of returning the $100 earnings to the shareholders. If the money is paid out as a dividend, then the personal tax bill will be $35, if the marginal tax rate of the equity holders is 35 percent. The net of tax receipts from the dividend is $65. The value of the company would return to $1000 or $10 per share after the dividend payment. On the other hand, if the firm used its $100 to buy 9.09 of its shares at a price of $11, then the total realized gain by those who sell their shares to the firm is $9.09, assuming that the sellers are among those who origi-

Table 1   EXAMPLE OF DIVIDEND PAYMENT AND SHARE REPURCHASE
FOR HYPOTHETICAL FIRM

Initial financing	100 shares		
Profit		$ 1/share	$ 100
Value at end of year		$11/share	$1,100
		Strategy A: $1 dividend payment/share	Strategy B: repurchase $100 worth of shares
Cash received by shareholders		$100	$100
Value of firm after transaction		$1,000	$1,000
Number of shares		100	90.91
Price per share		$10	$11
Taxes owed[a]		$35	$ 1.27
Accrued capital gain[b]		$ 0.00	$90.91

[a] Assumes personal tax rate of 35 percent and holding period of more than six months.
[b] Accrued capital gains will generate a future tax obligation if realized. A recent estimate of the effective tax rate on accrued capital gains is about 5 percent.

nally financed the firm at a $10 per share price, and the tax on that $9.09 would be at long-term capital gains rates. Under current law there is a 60 percent exclusion on long-term gains, so that only $3.64 would be subject to full personal taxation. If the appropriate tax rate were again 35 percent, that tax bill would amount to $1.27 and the stockholders would have net of tax proceeds of $98.73.

Note that in this example the company's shares remain at $11 after the repurchase and thus the remaining 90.91 shares each have an accrued gain of one dollar. These accrued gains will generate some taxes for the government, although the present value of those tax collections depends on average holding periods as well as the use of the escape of capital gains taxes that pass through estates.

This example highlights the much lower personal taxes that result from share repurchases relative to dividends. Even so, it still may exaggerate what would actually be paid with share repurchase. In the real world, investors have bought their shares at different times and at different prices, and those most likely to actually tender their shares back to the company will be those with the lowest reservation price on holding the shares. These most likely would be shareholders who have actually lost money on their investments, particularly those who have held the shares less than six months and who may be able to fully deduct their losses. This indicates that the government may actually get no immediate revenue from those who receive the corporate cash. The example also illustrates that even when the tax rate on realized capital gains was the same as that on dividends, the government's contemporaneous tax collections would be lower with share repurchase (because most of the money received is treated as a return of basis), as would the present value of its eventual tax receipts.

One interesting aspect of share repurchase is that shareholders are nearly indifferent to the price offered in a share repurchase plan, which is accomplished through a tender offer. The point is that in a fundamental way they are buying the shares from themselves, so the indifference comes from their being both buyer and seller. Consider what would happen to the above example if the firm offered to buy eight shares at $12.50 rather than 9.09 at $11.00. Shareholders as a group still get $100 cash, and the firm is still worth $1000 after the transaction. In some sense, there is a transfer between those who sell and those who do not if the firm pays an above-market price for the shares it recaptures, but this effect is diminished by the fact that if the offer is oversubscribed, the shares are repurchased from those who offer to sell on a pro rata basis. As long as all shareholders have an equal right to participate, then it is again hard to argue that there is a significant transfer among shareholders. There is a secondary tax difference. In the example of Table 1, the total realized capital gain would be $20 at the $12.50 price, whereas it was $9.09 at $11.00 per share.

Although I have emphasized the personal tax advantage of share repurchase, there are other reasons for this practice. One is that it is a mechanism for increasing the firm's debt-equity ratio. As mentioned above, the standard wisdom is that a firm's debt-equity ratio is determined by a tradeoff between the tax advantage of debt and the costs of its resulting inflexibility in times of crisis. However, if there is a change in the underlying riskiness of the firm (perhaps due to the maturing of a market or the resolution of some technological uncertainties), the firm may want to operate with a higher leverage ratio to enjoy the tax advantages of debt. Or, once the firm has achieved its desired debt-equity ratio, the stockmarket could increase the valuation of the shares and thus automatically lower leverage. The firm might want to counter the automatic unlevering that occurs with a rise in the stockmarket. Share repurchase can be a mechanism for increasing leverage. It may be a better mechanism for this transitional purpose than an increased dividend (suggested by the work of Feldstein and Green (1983)) because of the penalty that the market imposes on firms that subsequently cut their dividend.[2] Taken together with the previous observation that shareholders are approximately indifferent regarding the price of a share repurchase, this implies that a large increase in equity values, such as that of the past three years, may encourage share repurchases rather than discourage them, as seems to be the conventional wisdom.

Of course, the argument that share repurchases occur to implement an optimal debt-equity ratio is itself a tax-driven argument. In this case, it is the corporate tax faced by equity, rather than the personal tax that would accompany a dividend payment, that is being avoided by the absorption of equity.

Another reason that one might expect to observe firms buying back their own shares in preference to paying dividends is that doing so could be part of an antitakeover strategy (Simon (1986)). If a company pays cash out as a dividend, then the cash is given to all shareholders in proportion to their share holdings. However, if the cash is used to make a share repurchase tender offer, only those who tender their shares (or a pro rata proportion of those tendered) will receive cash from the firm. Due to different transactions costs, tax situations, and expectations about the firm's prospects there exists a distribution over prices at which

2. The fact that capital markets punish dividend cuts with large stock-price reductions is documented in Charest (1978), Aharony and Swary (1980), and Jensen (1986).

different shareholders are willing to sell. The cash dividend does not change that distribution, and the share repurchase buys out those with the lowest reservation prices, leaving behind those who would sell only when offered a premium above the tender offer price. Since a successful raider must obtain 51 percent of the outstanding shares, the fact that those with the lowest reservation prices have been taken out of the distribution by a share repurchase raises the cost of a takeover. This explanation is consistent with the empirical observation that merger activity and share repurchase have increased simultaneously in the last few years, although other theories might also explain both practices.

I assert that, in the absence of informational problems and transactions costs, buying the shares in another company is nearly equivalent to buying back your own shares. Rather than returning cash to the shareholders, the firm instead buys a financial investment. If the market value of the acquired asset is equal to what is paid for it (and there is no evidence that the rate of return on the common stock of the acquiring firm is abnormal, whereas there is an excess return enjoyed by the holders of the securities of the acquired firm (Dennis and McConnell (1986)), then in the absence of transactions costs the acquisition is as good as cash to the holders of the stock in the acquiring firm. If there are transactions costs, they would have to be taken into account, because some investors might now prefer cash and some investors might want to rebalance their portfolio after the acquisition.

Another way to note the near equivalence of cash mergers and share repurchase is to consider an example with two firms. The owners of firms A and B are nearly indifferent to whether both firms buy back 10 percent of their own stock or whether they buy 10 percent of each other. The cash flow to the investors is the same, the individual who owns a proportion of A + B is treated exactly equivalently, and the individual who owns either A or B has a claim of equal value. One qualifier is that if either A or B pays out dividends, then each corporation will face a tax on 15 percent of the dividends it receives from the other. Also, the proposition made above that shareholders are nearly indifferent regarding the price offered in a share repurchase tender offer program is clearly not true if the acquirer is an outside firm. Rather than the shareholders buying a fraction of outstanding shares from themselves, they now are selling them to an outsider, and therefore the common logic that the higher the price the better applies.

Cash mergers and leveraged buyouts (LBOs), much in the news of late, are just the complete purchase of all of the shares of a company by another company. They often involve large sums of money being paid from the corporate sector to stockholders and therefore are a significant determinant of the value of equity. In a merger or acquisition, the appreciation of the securities (which may reflect previous retained earnings) will be taxed as a capital gain rather than as ordinary income. Since in this case (unlike the situation with share repurchase) we are mainly comparing realized capital gains with dividends, the tax advantage of a cash merger will be diminished if the capital gains exclusion is eliminated, which now appears likely. However, a fraction of the money used for the acquisition will be a nontaxable return of basis.

So far, I have been arguing that there are significant tax advantages to paying out whatever cash is to be returned to equity investors in a form other than dividends. In this paper, I present data that indicate that most of the cash received by stockholders from firms in the last two years has been due to share repurchase and cash mergers. In 1985, at least $125 billion was paid out in share acquisitions, whereas dividends amounted to $83.5 billion. This phenomenon is relatively new, because in the first half of the 1970s the total money paid by corporations for equity acquisition amounted to only about 15 percent of dividends. I also demonstrate that the growth in share acquisitions is consistent with firms taking advantage of the tax treatment of debt in response to their increased market values.

The next section of the paper presents the data regarding the magnitude of these cash flows between firms and stockholders. The primary data source is the *Monthly stock returns file* of the Center for Research in Security Prices (CRSP). The second section of the paper examines where the money to make these payments comes from. One possibility is that they are directly substituting for dividends, and that dividends have declined as these practices have grown. This hypothesis is addressed by fitting aggregate time series equations for dividends and looking at the out-of-sample forecast residuals for recent years. Because funds are fungible, it is always difficult to be precise about where particular monies are coming from. Other possibilities in this case are that the money is being raised in debt markets and that effectively firms are changing their debt-equity ratios (in which case dividends and share repurchases are complements), or that declining industries are depreciating their capital in their traditional business and either returning the funds to their investors (share repurchase) or making investments on their behalf.

The third section addresses the question of what is the cost to the treasury of these nondividend cash payments. The answer depends on what firms would do if these payments were disallowed or taxed as dividends. If firms would pay these sums out to equity holders nonetheless, then the loss depends on the difference between the current taxation applying to these payments and their taxation as dividends. However, if they would retain these earnings and reduce borrowing, the loss is the present value of the future corporation income tax resulting from the higher level of corporate equity if these nondividend payments were not made. Both alternative scenarios are considered. The paper concludes in section 4 with an assessment of what we have learned regarding the nondividend payments to shareholders, and some speculation about how the new tax bill will affect these practices.

1. How Large Is It?

There is surprisingly little data regarding these nondividend cash payments between firms and stockholders, particularly share repurchases. There is no separate entry for them in the Federal Reserve's Flow of Funds accounts, and my contacts with the Fed have indicated that they do not have accurate information about this cash flow. There are some sources regarding mergers and acquisitions, and those figures are reported here.

To gain some feel for the magnitude of share repurchases, I examined the CRSP *Monthly stock returns file,* which contains monthly information on the number of shares outstanding. Only New York Stock Exchange (NYSE) securities were examined, and the period covered was January 1970 through December 1985. Each decrease in the number of shares outstanding (adjusted for splits and reverse splits) was taken to be a share repurchase, and the amount of cash represented by that share repurchase was determined by valuing the decrease in shares at the average of the price at the end of the preceding month and the price at the end of the month in which the reduction occurred. Overall, the sample covered 3,211 firms over 192 months.

The results of this procedure are shown in column 2 of Table 2. They show that the value of shares repurchased moved trendlessly between 1970 and 1976 at levels of approximately $2 billion or less. By 1980, the aggregate figure had grown to almost $8 billion, and it continued to grow rapidly, rising to more than $29 billion in 1984. There was a slight decline in 1985, although the figure of $27 billion is still very large.

For several reasons, the estimates of column 2 should be taken only as rough but very conservative estimates. First, only monthly *net* declines in shares outstanding are valued rather than the more appropriate, but unavailable, gross number of shares repurchased. The distinction should be made clear if you think of a firm that repurchases 100,000 shares but uses 50,000 of them to cover exercised executive stock options. The company shareholders receive cash for 100,000 of their shares, but the CRSP-based technique of this paper will only record that 50,000 shares were bought by the company.[3] By examining some 1985 and 1986 NYSE data on changes in Treasury stock for listed companies, I estimate that the valuation of net rather than gross stock repurchases may cause the figures of column 2 to be underestimated by as much as 20 percent.[4]

Second, only NYSE securities are covered in the procedure behind the figures in the first two columns of Table 2. Although they represent the vast majority of dividends, assets, and profits in the United States, the strategies being examined here, particularly share repurchase, are also likely to occur in small, closely held companies where possible informa-

3. For example, in the first quarter of 1985, IBM repurchased 1.575 million shares, but issued 1.35 million as part of defined contribution saving plans and stock options for employees.
4. This estimate is made by examining the monthly gross increases and decreases from Treasury stock in data made available by NYSE for 1985.

Table 2   VALUES OF MERGERS AND ACQUISITIONS, SHARE REPURCHASES, AND DIVIDENDS (MILLIONS OF CURRENT DOLLARS)

Year	Value of mergers and acquisitions (1)	Value of shares repurchased (2)	Dividends (3)
1970	2,824	1,213	22,500
1971	4,037	736	22,900
1972	2,407	2,121	24,400
1973	2,186	1,585	27,000
1974	2,215	2,059	29,700
1975	1,320	2,139	29,600
1976	5,324	1,904	34,600
1977	6,020	3,368	39,500
1978	7,660	5,804	44,700
1979	13,992	5,651	50,100
1980	19,845	7,802	54,700
1981	35,342	15,464	63,600
1982	36,322	11,700	66,900
1983	26,096	24,485	70,800
1984	62,690	29,098	78,100
1985	94,809	27,294	83,500

Sources: Column 1 contains the author's computations based on the CRSP tape. It represents the total value of firms that disappear from the NYSE, where value is determined by multiplying the number of shares outstanding the month before disappearance by the price at that time. Column 2 contains the author's computations based on the CRSP tape. It represents the sum of the value of all monthly decreases in the number of shares outstanding for NYSE stocks, where the value of the decrease in shares is determined by using the average of the price at the end of the preceding month and the price at the end of the month in which the reduction occurred. Column 3 is from the *Economic Report of the President*, February 1986, column 4, Table B-84, page 351.

tion problems relating to corporate financial behavior are much less severe than in large corporate giants.

Third, although CRSP offers accurate data on the change in the number of shares outstanding, I have no information on the price at which those shares were removed from the market. The procedures of using an average of the end of previous month's price and the price at the end of the month in which the repurchase occurred is probably downward biased. Those repurchase programs accomplished with a tender offer usually involve a premium above-market price and therefore involve more cash than the procedure of this paper will record.[5]

The first column of Table 2 contains information about mergers and acquisitions from the same sample of months and firms. The figures represent the value of shares of companies that disappear from the NYSE, where value is determined by multiplying the number of shares outstanding at the end of the month before disappearance by the price at that time. The results again show a series with no tendency to growth from 1970 to 1975. During that period, aggregate mergers and acquisitions averaged less than $2.5 billion compared to dividends, which averaged about $25 billion. By 1979, total mergers and acquisitions were almost $14 billion, and in 1985 they surpassed dividends by totaling almost $95 billion. In 1985, total dividends in the economy were only 68 percent as large as the value of NYSE mergers and share repurchases.

As with column 2, the figures of column 1 should be treated as rough approximations. They cover only NYSE securities; they do not include partial acquisitions; the price at which the shares are valued is certainly biased downwards in this case; and they do not separate cash from stock-swap mergers. In recent years, at least 83 percent of the largest mergers and acquisitions have used cash or equivalents rather than an equity exchange,[6] but it is difficult to summarize the magnitude of the bias in the figures in column 1. It is my personal assessment that the numbers are once again fairly conservative. The third column of Table 2 reports aggregate dividends of the corporate sector. It is an extremely stable series, as is well documented (Lintner (1956), Brittain (1966), and Shiller (1981)).

Figure 1 displays the same information, although now expressed in constant 1982 dollars, where the GNP deflator has been used to deflate

---

5. Dann (1981) says that "the tender offer price is usually higher than the market price at the time of the offer" (p. 114, footnote 3), and that although "open market repurchases occur more frequently than do tender offers to repurchase . . . [they] are generally of much smaller magnitude" (p. 115).
6. This calculation is the result of the comparison between total value and cash and equivalence of the 1985 *Mergers and Acquisitions* in Table 4.

the figures of Table 2. The figure clearly shows that both mergers and share repurchases were relatively insignificant until 1978, but since then they have experienced explosive growth.

Table 3 contains information on the twenty-five largest mergers and acquisitions in 1984, and Table 4 has the same information for 1985. The data were compiled by *Mergers and Acquisitions*. For 1984, the twenty-five largest deals amounted to almost half of the value of all mergers and acquisitions. Even the top twenty-five were dominated by the largest three, all involving oil companies buying other oil companies. The total cost of the acquisitions of Gulf, Getty, and Superior alone amounted to almost $30 billion, or nearly 25 percent of all such activity. Table 4 shows that no 1985 merger was as large as the three giant oil deals in 1984. However, total mergers and acquisitions were larger, with even the twenty-fifth largest deal amounting to $1 billion. Table 4 also shows that foreign investors became a major factor in equity mergers and acquisitions in 1985. The purchase of U.S. firms by non-U.S. firms went from $8 billion in 1984 to almost $18 billion in 1985. I note that the aggregate information

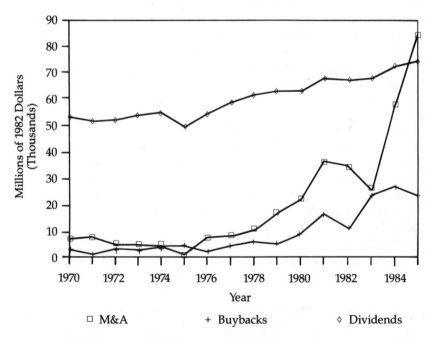

Figure 1   MERGERS, BUYBACKS, AND DIVIDENDS (In constant 1982 dollars)

Table 3   VALUE OF TWENTY-FIVE LARGEST COMPLETED MERGERS AND
ACQUISITIONS IN 1984

Acquiring company	Acquired company	Total value (million $)	Cash and equivalents (million $)
Chevron	Gulf	13,300.0	13,300.0
Texaco	Getty Oil	10,125.0	10,125.0
Mobil	Superior Oil	5,700.0	5,700.0
Kiewit-Murdock Invest.	Continental Group	2,750.0	2,750.0
Beatrice	Esmark	2,710.0	2,710.0
General Motors[a]	Electronic Data Sys.	2,600.7	2,600.7
Broken Hill	Utah International	2,400.0	2,400.0
Champion International	St. Regis	1,826.9	1,100.0
Phillips Petroleum	Energy subs. of RJR Ind.	1,700.0	1,700.0
Manufacturers Hanover	C.I.T. Financial	1,510.0	1,510.0
Dun & Bradstreet	A. C. Nielson	1,339.0	0.0
IBM	ROLM	1,260.0	1,260.0
Pace Industries	Part of City Invest.	1,251.0	1,251.0
American General	Ins. subs. Gulf United	1,200.0	0.0
American Stores	Jewel	1,150.0	0.0
J. W. K. Acquisition Co.	Metromedia	1,130.0	1,130.0
Penn Central	14.5% Gulf	1,110.0	811.0
General Electric	Employers Reinsurance	1,075.0	1,075.0
Texas Eastern	Petrolane	1,040.0	1,040.0
Kohlbery, Kravis, Roberts	Wometco Enterprises	977.4	842.0
Schlumberger	SEDCO Inc.	958.7	431.0
ARA Holding Co.	ARA Services	882.5	882.5
American Medical Intl.	Lifemark	863.0	0.0
American Express	Invest. Divers. Service	774.6	373.7
Gulf & Western	Prentice-Hall	705.3	705.3
Total value of 25 largest completed mergers and acquisitions		60,340.0	53,697.2
Value of all mergers and acquisitions between U.S. firms		114,996.8	
Non-U.S. firms acquiring U.S. firms		8,207.2	
U.S. firms acquiring non-U.S. firms		2,024.8	
Total value of all mergers and acquisitions		125,228.8	

Cash and equivalents include cash, bonds and debentures, and preferred stock. The figures shown are lower-bound estimates of cash and equivalents.

[a] EDS stockholders had an option to exchange stock instead of cash.

Sources: First three columns, *Mergers and Acquisitions* 19, no. 5 (May/June 1985). Fourth column, various issues of *Mergers and Acquisitions* and the *Value Line Investment Survey.*

Table 4   VALUE OF TWENTY-FIVE LARGEST COMPLETED MERGERS AND
ACQUISITIONS IN 1985

Acquiring company	Acquired company	Total value (million $)	Cash and equivalents (million $)
Royal Dutch Shell	Shell Oil	5.670.0	5,670.0
Phillip Morris	General Foods	5,627.6	5,627.6
General Motors	Hughes Aircraft	5,025.0	2,700.0
R. J. Reynolds	Nabisco Brands	4,904.5	4,904.5
Allied Corp.	Signal Cos.	4,850.8	1,000.0
Baxter Travenol[a]	Amer. Hosp. Supply	3,702.6	3,702.6
Nestle SA	Carnation	2,893.6	2,893.6
Monsanto	G. D. Searle	2,717.1	2,717.1
Coastal Corp.	Amer. Nat. Resources	2,454.4	2,454.4
InterNorth	Houston Natural Gas	2,260.4	*
MacAndrews & Forbes	Revlon	1,741.6	1,741.6
Kohlberg, Kravis, Roberts	Union Texas Petrol.	1,700.0	1,700.0
Rockwell International	Allen-Bradley	1,651.0	1,651.0
SCI Holdings	Storer Communications	4,196.7	1,491.9
Textron Inc.	Avco Corp.	1,380.0	1,380.0
Cooper Industries	McGraw-Edison	1,377.0	1,100.0
Cox Enterprises	Cox Communications	1,265.2	1,265.2
Proctor & Gamble	Richardson-Vicks	1,245.7	1,245.7
Midcon Corp.	United Energt. Res.	1,241.9	742.0
Chesebrough-Ponds	Stauffer Chemical	1,218.0	1,218.0
Farley Industries	Northwest Industries	1,158.5	1,158.5
HHF Corp.	Levi Strauss	1,110.0	1,110.1
Wickes Corp.	Parts of Gulf & Western	1,073.0	1,000.0
Mesa Partners II	13.6% of Unocal	1,052.0	1,052.0
Management led	MGIC Investment	1,000.0	*
Total value of 25 largest completed mergers and acquisitions		59,816.7	49,525.8
Value of all mergers and acquisitions between U.S. firms		120,217.9	
Non-U.S. firms acquiring U.S. firms		17,793.1	
U.S. firms acquiring non-U.S. firms		1,115.2	
Total value of all mergers and acquisitions		139,126.2	

Cash and equivalents include cash, bonds and debentures, and preferred stock. The figures shown are lower-bound estimates of cash and equivalents.

*Details regarding merger terms could not be determined.

[a] American Hospital Supply stockholders had an option to exchange stock instead of cash.

Sources: First three columns, Mergers and Acquisitions 20, no. 5 (May/June 1986). Fourth column, various issues of Mergers and Acquisitions and the Value Line Investment Survey.

shown for 1984 and 1985 in Tables 3 and 4 exceeds the corresponding figures in Table 2 and Figure 1. Part of the explanation is that the *Mergers and Acquisitions* data of Tables 3 and 4 include partial acquisitions, non-NYSE firms, and even non-U.S. firms. However, I do not mean to imply that the two sources could be exactly reconciled. On the other hand, both indicate the same order of magnitude for the value of mergers and acquisitions.

Table 5 shows the twenty-five largest share repurchase programs for 1985. The list was generated by identifying the forty-five firms with the largest net share acquisition programs from the CRSP file and augment-

Table 5   VALUE OF TWENTY-FIVE LARGEST SHARE REPURCHASE PROGRAMS IN 1985

Company	Total value of shares repurchased (million $)
Phillips Petroleum	4,500
Unocal	4,178
Arco	3,100
Exxon	2,748
Litton Ind.	1,320
Westinghouse	975
CBS	955
AMOCO	742
Revlon Inc.	575
Scott Paper	546
PPG Inds. Inc.	530
Chrysler Corp.	472
Times Mirror Co.	459
Pepsico	458
Ford Motor	449
R. J. Reynolds	403
Mapco Inc.	398
Coca Cola	380
Colgate Palmolive	371
Eastman Kodak	353
Knight Ridder Newspapers	334
Raytheon	333
Santa Fe Southern Pacific Corp.	302
Consolidated Edison Co. NY Inc.	289
General Electric	283

Source: The values of shares repurchased were obtained from SEC 10-K filings and annual reports for 1985. We considered as potential candidates firms evidencing large repurchase by either of two sources: being amongst the forty-five largest as derived by our CRSP manipulations, or having significant increases in the shares of Treasury stock holdings, and thus repurchase value, as obtained by our NYSE Treasury stock report manipulations.

ing that sample by those firms whose share repurchase programs appear to be large in the NYSE data. The annual reports and Securities and Exchange Commission (SEC) 10-K forms for all of these firms were examined, and the values here are derived from these reports. The oil companies are extremely prominent on the list, as they are on the mergers and acquisitions tables already given. The oil companies were experiencing large cash flows due to the high price of crude, but had excess capacity in refining because the high prices had reduced demand. This "cash-cow" situation is exactly the type of situation where one would expect the firm to transmit cash or value to shareholders by a nondividend technique. Exxon alone repurchased more than $5 billion of its shares in 1984 and 1985, a sum exceeding Exxon's dividends for the same two years. The non–oil companies on the list also appear to be mature companies in slow growth industries. In subsequent research, I intend to examine econometrically the determinants of which firms are most likely to engage in repurchase programs.

The overall conclusion that I reach from the data gathered so far is that nondividend forms of payment have been growing rapidly, now exceed dividends in aggregate, and that this may be a mechanism for investment to be reallocated away from slow growth sectors of the economy to other areas offering higher growth. In this regard, note that even when one oil company absorbs another with a cash merger, some cash is reallocated out of the industry because equity holders receive cash from the acquiring firm, which they then can reallocate in whatever manner they choose.

2. Have Firms Reduced Dividends?

Corporations are now paying out over $100 billion per year in nondividend cash to equity holders. At some level it is impossible to track down the origins of that money, since the interchangeability of funds renders it fundamentally impossible to match sources and uses. However, it still is interesting to investigate what other behavior has accompanied the growth in cash flows from share absorption.

The first source suspected might be dividends. If it has become recognized that share repurchases and cash mergers are tax-preferred relative to dividends, then one would expect dividends to have declined as these practices have grown. It has long been known that aggregate dividends are a very smooth series, with dividend levels adjusting to changes in earnings with fairly long lags (see, for example, Lintner (1956), Brittain (1966), and Auerbach (1982)).

I wish to test this substitutability hypothesis. Thus, I have fit simple partial-adjustment models similar to those used by Auerbach (1982). In the equations in Table 6, dividends depend on the previous year's dividends, profits, a correction for the real inflation-adjusted cost of debt, and q (the ratio of the financial valuation of the firm to the replacement cost of its assets).[7] Three alternative specifications are estimated.

The 1960–1982 aggregate data used in the estimations are shown in Table 6. The resulting estimated equations are then used to predict the level of dividends in 1983 and 1984. The results strongly suggest that the

Table 6   ALTERNATIVE MODELS OF CORPORATE DIVIDEND BEHAVIOR (ANNUAL DATA 1960–1982)

Independent variable	Dependent variable: Dividends		
	Equation 1	Equation 2	Equation 3
Intercept	3.78	9.80	7.16
	(0.73)[a]	(1.48)	(1.18)
Dividends (lagged)	0.80	0.88	0.84
	(6.97)	(9.80)	(7.84)
Profits (adjusted after tax)	0.06	—	0.06
	(2.47)		(2.45)
Inflation gain on new debt	0.09	—	−0.03
	(0.85)		(−0.21)
q	—	−2.04	−3.96
		(−0.75)	(−1.07)
R^{-2}	0.89	0.86	0.89
Durbin-Watson statistic	1.59	1.65	1.94

		Out of sample predictions: Dividends		
Year	Actual	Equation 1	Predicted equation 2	Equation 3
1983	68.2	66.3 [2.8][b]	66.9 [1.9]	67.5 [1.1]
1984	72.2	68.0[a] [5.8]	66.9 [7.4]	69.8 [2.6]
		69.6[d] [3.7]	68.0 [5.8]	70.4 [2.6]
1985	74.8	—	66.7[c] [11.0]	—
		—	71.4[d] [4.5]	—

[a] T-statistics in parentheses.

[b] Percentage prediction error in brackets.

[c] Using predicted lagged dividends.

[d] Using actual lagged dividends.

source of the cash is not a lowering of dividends. All three specifications of the dividend equation continue to track dividends rather well, with the residuals in 1983 and 1984 always being positive. This indicates that dividends were slightly higher than the equations would have forecasted. Equations 1 and 3 show profits to be a significant variable in determining dividends. The long-run equilibrium payout rate out of inflation-adjusted profits ranges from 30 to 37.5 percent. Of course, the stability of dividends and the market penalty for failing to fulfill expectations regarding dividends is well known. Once the practice of paying dividends and periodically increasing them is established, the market makes it difficult to not satisfy this expectation.

Despite the cash payouts for share acquisition, the total sources of funds raised or generated by the corporate sector have continued to increase in the last few years. Total internal cash generated in the corporate sector increased 66 percent between 1981 and 1985, going from $213 billion to almost $355 billion (Board of Governors of the Federal Reserve System (1981)). This increase alone is more than sufficient to account for the increase in equity absorption. The fungibility point made earlier is highlighted when one notes that the corporate sector has been increasing its bond and bank debts by over $100 billion per year in the last several years. This source is also large enough to fund the share acquisitions.

The available aggregate information weakly supports the hypothesis that firms are repurchasing equity with debt-financed funds to achieve their target leverage ratios. The aggregate debt-equity ratio of U.S. corporations in 1984 and 1985 was approximately the same as it had been in 1979–1981, despite the large increase in equity values. The aggregate figures compiled by Salomon Brothers are shown in Table 7. They show that U.S. corporations have been on average absorbing equity and issu-

Table 7 DEBT AND EQUITY FOR U.S. CORPORATIONS (BILLION $)

	Net new debt	Total value of debt at year end	Net stock issuance	Stock appreciation	Total value of corporate stock at year end	Debt-equity ratio
1980	38.6	418.8	11.6	381.2	1,572.3	.266
1981	30.4	449.2	−23.5	−43.8	1,505.0	.298
1982	48.0	497.2	−20.3	236.4	1,721.1	.289
1983	46.2	543.4	25.8	275.3	2,022.3	.269
1984	80.8	624.2	−82.8	82.7	2,378.2	.262

Source: *Prospects for financial markets, 1980–1985*. New York: Salomon Brothers.

ing debt, so the net effect has been relatively constant leverage rates, despite the rally in equity market values.

3. *How Much Does It Cost?*

The next question I address is how much does the Treasury lose because of the use of nondividend forms of payment between firms and their stockholders. It is a somewhat difficult issue for several reasons. Fundamentally, we do not know what the firm would have done if share repurchase and cash mergers were disallowed. One possibility is that it would increase dividends as the only remaining mechanism to absorb equity in establishing its desired debt-equity ratio. Of course, the optimal debt-equity ratio itself is a function of the tax laws. A second possibility is that the funds would be retained in the corporation, and the firm's new borrowing would have been reduced. Either of these possibilities implies that share repurchase and acquisition cost the Treasury large amounts of tax revenue. I will assess this cost for these two scenarios.

If the alternative would have been an equal amount of payments as dividends, the revenue loss to the Treasury is the difference between the average marginal tax rate on dividends and the effective tax rate on the share purchase cash payments. The average marginal tax rate applying to dividend distributions depends on several factors. First, within households, some will have not used up the $100 per person ($200 per couple) dividend exclusion. Second, one would expect that people would arrange their portfolios such that those with low marginal tax rates hold assets that are heavily taxed (e.g., stocks that offer high dividend yields, such as utilities), whereas those with high marginal tax rates would hold more lightly taxed securities (such as companies that retain earnings or repurchase shares or, at the extreme, municipal bonds). Certainly, these clientele effects exist, although their empirical strength is somewhat uncertain.[8] Of course, substantial amounts of equity are held by insurance companies, pension funds, and nonprofit institutions, which are not taxed. Feldstein and Jun (1986) have estimated a time series of the effective average marginal tax rates on dividends, taking into account the

---

7. The partial adjustment model can be represented as $D_t - D_{t-1} = \lambda(D_t^* - D_{t-1})$, where D_t is dividends for year t and D_t^* is the long-run equilibrium or desired level of dividends. D^* is assumed to depend on corporate profits corrected for inflation (i.e., with the capital consumption adjustments, inventory valuation adjustment, and a recognition of the gain on the net corporate debt due to inflation) and q.

8. The clientele effect was originally suggested by Modigliani and Miller (1961) and has been quantified by Elton and Gruber (1970), and Pettit (1977).

proportion of stocks held by households, insurance companies, and nontaxable holders. Their series is reproduced as the second column of Table 8. Using these rates, it is rather simple to determine how much tax would have been paid if these nondividend payments to stockholders continued and were taxed as dividends, or if companies replaced them with increased dividends.[9] However, to know how much extra the government would collect, we must know how much tax was collected from these payments in the current situation.

The effective tax rate applying to the nondividend cash payments under current law is undoubtedly quite low. As demonstrated in the example of Table 1, share repurchases create a capital gain of equivalent magnitude to the cash payment of dividends, but most of that capital gain is accrued rather than realized. Most of the money received by the

---

9. This assumes that the effective average marginal tax rate for the pool of firms using repurchase is the same as for the market at large. We will not consider issues of self-selection here.

Table 8   LOSS IN TAX REVENUES DUE TO NONDIVIDEND CASH PAYMENTS ASSUMING ALTERNATIVE IS INCREASED DIVIDENDS

Year	Tax rate on dividends	Additional taxes on cash mergers (million $)	Additional taxes on share repurchases (million $)	Total additional taxes (million $)
1970	0.339	816.0	350.6	1,166.6
1971	0.338	1,162.6	212.0	1,374.6
1972	0.327	666.7	587.6	1,254.4
1973	0.319	587.9	426.4	1,014.3
1974	0.323	604.7	562.1	1,166.8
1975	0.322	359.1	581.8	940.8
1976	0.333	1,506.6	538.9	2,045.5
1977	0.343	1,763.9	986.9	2,750.8
1978	0.346	2,267.2	1,717.8	3,985.1
1979	0.360	4,337.6	1,751.7	6,089.4
1980	0.359	6,132.0	2,410.7	8,542.7
1981	0.358	10,885.4	4,762.9	15,648.3
1982	0.301	9,116.8	2,936.7	12,053.6
1983	0.285	6,132.6	5,753.9	11,886.5
1984	0.275	14,105.2	6,547.0	20,652.2
1985	0.275	21,332.0	6,141.2	27,473.2

Sources: Tax rate on dividends column was taken from column 3, Table A-4, of Feldstein and Jun (1986). Additional tax revenues were derived by multiplying the magnitudes in columns 1 and 2 of Table 1 by the tax rate on dividends less 5 percent. The 5 percent represents the effective marginal tax rate on accrued capital gains and is roughly consistent with Protopapadakis (1983).

actual sellers is a return of basis, with the remainder being taxed at capital gains rates. Under current law, only 40 percent of realized long-term capital gains are taxed. The effective rate of taxation on accrued gains is much lower, due to deferral and the fact that the gains on assets that pass through estates completely escape taxation. A recent times series of estimates of effective marginal tax rates on accrued capital gains that took these considerations into account put those rates between 4 and 6 percent (Protopapadakis (1983)).

The tax situation with cash mergers is similar to share repurchase. Relative to the payment of a dividend, the holders of the acquiring company experience an accrued capital gain. The owners of the acquired company pay capital gains taxes on the appreciation of their securities, but again the majority of the money received is usually a nontaxed return of basis. With this background, I have assumed that the tax rate applicable to the nondividend cash flows was 5 percent over the entire 1970–1985 period. This is consistent with Protopapadakis's estimates, and small errors in this figure are relatively insignificant compared with the magnitude of the tax rate on dividends in Table 8.

With these tax rate assumptions, Table 8 indicates that the practice of share acquisition costs the government very little between 1970 and 1975 (roughly $1 billion per year), but that its cost has risen sharply since then, to more than $27 billion in 1985. This assumes that the alternative to acquisition is the increase of dividend payments. Interestingly, this $27 billion per year exceeds the intended shift between the personal and corporate taxation in the new tax bill. This exercise provides one indication of how the adjustment of household and firm behavior can significantly affect revenue projections from any proposed change of incentives in the tax code.

In the previous section, we found that dividends have not declined relative to equity earnings; thus it can be argued that dividends are not likely to be the behavior that is depressed as a result of share acquisition. What may be depressed is the outstanding quantity of corporate equity. If share purchases effectively reduce equity and increase debt (i.e., if the acquisitions are financed by borrowing), then the Treasury loses in present-value terms much more than is reflected in Table 8. The loss is not immediate, but results from the lower future corporation income tax receipts. By absorbing equity, the corporate sector is escaping from the double taxation imposed on equity. This opportunity exists because the corporate tax applied only to equity investments, since interest is deductible.

At a marginal corporate income tax rate of 46 percent, the value of the government's equity claim on an extra dollar's worth of earnings is 85 percent as large as the value of the claim of the investors. The government gains 46 cents from a marginal dollar of pretax profit, and the company keeps 54 cents.[10]

Table 9 shows the loss in present-value terms of the Treasury's tax receipts, under the assumption that share acquisition programs have reduced corporate equity. The figures indicate that the loss to the Treasury is insignificant before 1975, but exceeds $100 billion in 1985. That is, the absorption of corporate equity that occurred in 1985 reduces the present value of the corporate tax receipts by slightly more than $100 billion. The annual loss is much lower than this, perhaps only $5 billion. This table assumes that the personal tax bill is equivalent for corporate debt and equity, and that the transfer of capital between the two forms simply cuts

10. The Treasury's claim may be worth more than 85 percent of the value of the investor's claim, since the fifty-four cents faces further taxation at the personal level.

Table 9 LOSS IN THE PRESENT VALUE OF TAX REVENUES DUE TO NONDIVIDEND CASH PAYMENTS ASSUMING ALTERNATIVE IS LESS BORROWING

Year	Corporate tax rate on pretax earnings	Effective corporate tax rate on posttax earnings	Loss in present value of taxes due to cash mergers	Loss in present value of taxes due to share repurchases	Total present value loss in tax collection
1970	.492	.9685	2,734.625	1,175.036	3,909.661
1971	.480	.923	3,725.897	679.460	4,405.357
1972	.480	.923	2,221.660	1,958.112	4,179.772
1973	.480	.923	2,017.360	1,462.926	3,480.286
1974	.480	.923	2,044.462	1,900.572	3,945.034
1975	.480	.923	1,218.488	1,974.106	3,192.594
1976	.480	.923	4,913.642	1,757.588	6,671.230
1977	.480	.923	5,556.678	3,108.917	8,665.595
1978	.480	.923	7,069.812	5,356.655	2,426.467
1979	.460	.852	11,921.454	4,814.445	16,735.899
1980	.460	.852	16,907.578	6,647.019	23,554.597
1981	.460	.852	30,111.670	13,175.314	43,286.984
1982	.460	.852	30,946.398	9,968.533	40,914.931
1983	.460	.852	22,234.051	20,860.831	43,094.882
1984	.460	.852	53,411.811	24,791.368	78,203.179
1985	.460	.852	80,777.070	23,254.706	104,031.776

Sources: Column 1 is column 7 of Table B1 of Feldstein and Jun (1986).
Column 2 is column 1/(1 − column 1).
Column 3 is column 2 times column 1 of Table 2.
Column 4 is column 2 times column 2 of Table 2.

corporate collections. Although the tax rates faced by households on the return to debt may exceed the rates on equity return, a large fraction of debt is held in tax sheltered investments such as pension funds.

Each of the two hypotheses indicates that the Treasury losses are extremely large due to these practices. The former theory implies that the government is losing tax on dividends, and the latter suggests that it is losing corporation income tax revenue. Relative to models that do not incorporate behavioral change, each of the alternative hypotheses suggests massive revenue effects.

4. Conclusion

Corporations in the United States are now making nondividend cash payments to shareholders, the sum of which exceeds that of dividends. These payments have not received much attention by research economists, but their growth in magnitude challenges the conventional model of share valuation and certainly affects estimates of the taxes collected on corporate source income.

Share acquisitions (both share repurchase and cash mergers) may well be motivated by tax minimizing behavior. There are two potential sources of tax savings from these activities. First, if because of share acquisition dividends are lower than they otherwise would have been, then there is a tax saving at the personal level. With share acquisition by corporations, most of the cash returned to shareholders is a return of basis. The magnitude of the taxable capital gain depends on the form of the share acquisition. In the case of a firm repurchasing its own shares, most of the resulting capital gains are accrued rather than realized. The deferral advantage of accrued capital gain will continue to exist even when realized capital gains are fully taxed under the new federal law.

The second tax motivation for share acquisition is simply to escape the double taxation of equity. Both dividends and share acquisition eliminate equity. The tax saving results from the fact that equity earnings are subject to the corporation income tax, whereas debt interest is not. Because the market expects increases in dividends to be sustained, repurchase is an attractive mechanism to decrease equity. The tax advantage of leverage will continue with the new tax law.

A leading model of optimal financial policy has firms balancing the tax advantages of debt against the increased chance of incurring bankruptcy costs. The tremendous rise in equity values of the past three years may have given firms a capacity to carry more debt and absorb some equity. This hypothesis is consistent with the observations of explosive growth in noncash payments to equity holders and the fact that dividends are, if anything, also greater than their historic pattern.

In corporate behavior and tax policy evaluations, it is almost certainly useful to know what is happening. In 1985, corporations purchased well over $100 billion of equities, and, in present-value terms, this may cost the U.S. Treasury as much as $100 billion. Clearly, there has been a major change in corporate financial behavior that necessitates future research.

REFERENCES

Aharony, Joseph, and Itzhak Swary. 1980. Quarterly dividend and earnings announcements and stockholder's returns: An empirical analysis. *Journal of Finance* 35: 1–12.

Auerbach, Alan J. 1982. Issues in the measurement and encouragement of business saving. Saving and Government Policy, Conference Series No. 25, Federal Reserve Bank of Boston, 79–100.

Auerbach, Alan J. 1983. Taxation, corporate financial policy and the cost of capital. *Journal of Economic Literature* 21 (September): 905–40.

Board of Governors of the Federal Reserve System. 1986. *Balance Sheets for the U.S. Economy 1946–85.* Washington, D.C.: Flow of Funds (April).

Brittain, John A. 1966. *Corporate dividend policy.* Washington, D.C.: The Brookings Institution.

Center for Research in Security Prices. 1985. *CRSP monthly stock returns file.* Chicago: University of Chicago.

———. 1985. *CRSP monthly stock index file.* Chicago: University of Chicago.

Charest, Guy. 1978. Dividend information, stock returns, and market efficiency II. *Journal of Financial Economics* 6: 297–330.

Dann, Larry Y. 1981. Common stock repurchases. *Journal of Financial Economics* 9: 113–38.

Dennis, Debra K., and John J. McConnell. 1986. Corporate mergers and security returns. *Journal of Financial Economics* 16, no. 2 (June): 143–87.

Eades, Kenneth M., Patrick J. Hess, and E. Han Kim. 1984. On interpreting security returns during the ex-dividend period. *Journal of Financial Economics* 13: 3–34.

Economic Advisers, Council of. 1986. *Economic Report of the President.* Washington, D.C.: U.S. Government Printing Office (February).

Elton, E. J., and M. J. Gruber. 1970. Marginal stockholders' tax rates and the clientele effect. *Review of Economics and Statistics* (February): 68–74.

Fama, E., and H. Babiak. 1968. Dividend policy: An empirical analysis. *Journal of American Statistics Association* (December): 1132–61.

Fama, E., L. Fisher, M. Jensen, and R. Roll. 1969. The adjustment of stock prices to new information. *International Economic Review* (February): 1–21.

Feldstein, Martin, and Jerry Green. 1983. Why do companies pay dividends? *American Economic Review* 73, no. 1 (March): 17–30.

Feldstein, Martin, and Joosung Jun. 1986. The effects of tax rules on nonresidential fixed investment: Some preliminary evidence from the 1980s. NBER Working Paper no. 1857 (March).

Gordon, Roger H. 1982. Interest rates, inflation, and corporate financial policy. *Brookings Papers on Economic Activity* 2: 461–91.

Jensen, Michael C. 1986. The takeover controversy: Analysis and evidence. University of Rochester Working Paper no. MERC 86-01 (July).

———. 1986. Agency costs of free cash flow, corporate finance and takeovers. *American Economic Review* 76, no. 2 (May): 323–29.

Jensen, Michael C., and William Meckling. 1976. Theory of the firm: Managerial behavior, agency costs, and ownership structures. *Journal of Financial Economics* 3: 305–60.

Kim, E. H. 1978. A mean variance theory of optimal capital structure and corporate debt capacity. *Journal of Finance* (March): 45–64.

Kraus, A., and R. Litzenberger. 1973. A state-preference model of optimal financial leverage. *Journal of Finance* (September): 911–22.

Lintner, John. 1956. Distribution of incomes of corporations among dividends, retained earnings, and taxes. *American Economic Review* 46, no. 2 (May): 97–118.

Long, J. B., Jr. 1978. The market valuation of cash dividends: A case to consider. *Journal of Financial Economics* 6, no. 2/3 (June/September): 235–64.

Masulis, Ronald W. 1980. Stock purchase by tender offer: An analysis of the causes of common stock price changes. *Journal of Finance* 35, no. 2 (May): 305–21.

Mergers and Acquisitions, 1984 and 1985.

Miller, Merton H. 1977. Debt and taxes. *Journal of Finance* 32, no. 2 (May): 261–75.

Miller, Merton H., and Myron S. Scholes. 1978. Dividends and taxes. *Journal of Financial Economics* 6: 333–64.

Miller, Merton H., and Kevin Rock. 1984. Dividend policy under asymmetric information. Chicago: University of Chicago. Unpublished manuscript.

Modigliani, Franco. 1982. Debt, dividend policy, taxes, inflation and mixed valuation. Presidential Address, *Journal of Finance* 37 (May): 255–73.

Modigliani, F., and M. H. Miller. 1958. The cost of capital, corporation finance and the theory of investment. *American Economic Review* (June): 261–97.

———. 1961. Dividend policy, growth and the valuation of shares. *Journal of Business* 34 (October): 411–33.

———. 1963. Corporate income taxes and the cost of capital. *American Economic Review* (June): 433–43.

New York Stock Exchange, Inc. 1985. Treasury stock report (January–December).

———. 1986. Treasury stock report (January–May).

Ofer, Aharon R., and Anjan V. Thakor. 1986. A theory of stock price responses to alternative corporate cash disbursement methods: Stock repurchases and dividends. KGSM Northwestern and Indiana Business. Unpublished manuscript (August).

Pettit, R. R. 1977. Taxes, transactions costs and clientele effects of dividends. *Journal of Financial Economics* (December): 419–36.

Protopapadakis, Aris. 1983. Some indirect evidence on effective capital gains tax rates. *Journal of Business* 56, no. 2: 127–38.

Salomon Brothers Inc. 1980–1985. *Prospects for financial markets, 1980–1985.* New York.

Schaeffer, S. 1982. Tax-induced clientele effects in the market for British Government securities. *Journal of Financial Economics:* 121–59.

Schipper, K., and R. Thompson. 1983. The impact of merger-related regulations on the shareholders of acquiring firms. *Journal of Accounting Research:* 184–221.

Schleiffer, Andrei. 1986. Do demand curves for stocks slope down? *Journal of Finance* 41, no. 3: 579–90.

Shiller, R. J. 1981. Do stock prices move too much to be justified by subsequent changes in dividends? *American Economic Review* 71 (June): 421–36.

Simon, Laurie B. 1986. Share repurchase and the deterence of merger. Stanford, Calif.: Stanford University. Unpublished manuscript (September).

Stiglitz, J. 1972. Some aspects of the pure theory of corporate finance: Bankruptcies and takeovers. *Bell Journal of Economics and Management Science* (Autumn): 458–82.

Summers, Lawrence H. 1981. Taxation and corporate investment: A q-theory approach. *Brookings Papers on Economic Activity* 1: 67–140.

Tobin, James. 1969. A general equilibrium approach to monetary theory. *Journal of Money, Credit and Banking:* 15–29.

Vermaelen, Theo. 1981. Common stock repurchases and market signalling: An empirical study. *Journal of Financial Economics* (June): 139–83.

Williamson, O. E. 1971. The vertical integration of production: Market failure considerations. *American Economic Review* (May): 112–23.

Herman B. Leonard and Richard J. Zeckhauser

John F. Kennedy School of Government, Harvard University, and NBER,
John F. Kennedy School of Government, Harvard University, and NBER

Amnesty, Enforcement, and Tax Policy

Massachusetts raised $85 million through a tax amnesty program; New York collected more than four times that amount. In California, Illinois, Alabama, Arizona, Wisconsin, and twelve other states, people and corporations willingly stood in line for hours to pay the taxes they owed while delinquency penalties were temporarily suspended, to deliver bills and checks and coins to state treasuries. Many were choosing to make a first appearance on the tax rolls.

Tax amnesties have raised hundreds of millions of dollars that revenue collectors would otherwise have found difficult or impossible to capture. Amnesties have swelled the rolls of paid-up taxpayers and increased the population of regular filers. State revenue department estimates suggest that a well-publicized amnesty combined with stricter future enforcement considerably increases the level of future voluntary compliance with tax laws.

Amnesties may have had some less positive effects as well. They may have angered law-abiding taxpayers who dislike seeing tax breaks given to abusers of the system. Current amnesties may have encouraged some citizens to believe that there will be future amnesties as well, reducing their incentives to keep current on their payments. Not surprisingly, considerable controversy has arisen over whether (and how) tax policy should make use of amnesty programs.

In practice, tax amnesties have been coupled with enhanced enforce-

The authors are indebted to a great many people for insightful and useful comments they received. We would particularly like to thank Howard Frant, Arthur Gelber, Grady Hedgespeth, Ira Jackson, Nancy Jackson, Robert Landman, Allen Lerman, Larry Summers, and Diane Ukraine. No implied responsibility is transferred with our thanks.

ment efforts, a feature that seems essential to preserve the legitimacy of the tax code. (Moreover, given some factions' opposition to any reductions of penalties, the promise of more vigorous enforcement is probably necessary to win political approval of an amnesty program.) An amnesty and enforcement program twists the schedule of expected tax penalties, lowering them temporarily but raising them later, thus providing a strong incentive for offenders to come forward. An important further effect is to make future compliance more attractive. Citizens who have past delinquencies to conceal may hesitate to file an accurate current return lest it raise questions about previous years. But once the slate has been wiped clean under an amnesty program, their cost of future compliance is reduced.

Should the federal government follow the example of the states and offer a tax amnesty of its own? Today, when unprecedented federal budget deficits have reached 5 percent of gross national product (GNP), and many believe that tax evasion is costing the government as much as $100 billion a year, this question seems increasingly worthy of attention. Barring massive increases in enforcement expenditures, an amnesty might be the only way to bring many evaders back into compliance. Congress's recent approval of a sweeping tax reform, designed in part to restore legitimacy to the tax code, provides an opportune time to consider a federal tax amnesty coupled with more vigorous enforcement to capitalize on and help mark a new regime.

Some observers have argued that the decision whether to offer an amnesty should be based on a fairly mechanical weighing of additional tax collections to be achieved now against possible losses later. Such an approach, which in effect considers an amnesty program purely as a revenue-raising device, would be most appropriate if the program could be expected to raise a significant fraction of tax revenues, say 3 or 4 percent of total collections. Existing estimates, none of which claims to be more than speculation, are less optimistic. Allen H. Lerman, of the Office of Tax Analysis, U.S. Department of the Treasury, suggests that an amnesty might raise $1 billion (not including revenue due to greater future enforcement). Our assessment suggests that a combined amnesty/enforcement program—which political forces may make an inevitable coupling—could raise as much as $10 billion over the status quo, but even that sum would be only about 1.5 percent of revenues. To judge the virtues of an amnesty, policy makers will have to weigh the revenues raised against its other consequences, both positive and negative, which may be substantial. For example, some elements of a tax amnesty will support, and other elements will undermine, the legitimacy of the tax system and therefore the revenues that it collects. Given the salience of taxes in the citizen's interactions with the government, a tax amnesty may also affect the perceived overall legitimacy of government.

Many state amnesties have been accompanied by a significant strengthening of enforcement efforts. The revenues thus generated must be viewed as a product of the joint instrument. How then should we assess the efficacy of a prospective federal amnesty? Should we consider merely the effects of adding an amnesty, leaving present enforcement efforts unchanged? Or should we compare the status quo with an amnesty program that also includes a stepped-up enforcement program? Or should we assume a strict enforcement program and see what an amnesty adds?

In our view, an amnesty is a political instrument, a compromising counterbalance that helps lead to stricter enforcement efforts. (Indeed, Congress may never find time for a consequential discussion of enforcement except in the context of debate over a federal amnesty.) Thus a federal amnesty, together with the enforcement efforts likely to accompany it, should be judged against the realistic alternative, the enforcement expected without an amnesty. Moreover, to assess the full effects of an amnesty on revenue, we must consider the future impact of the accompanying enforcement changes. The experience of the states, as we shall see, suggests that enhanced future revenues exceed the direct revenues of the amnesty itself. Any revenue projections must remain highly speculative, however, making it all the more important to examine the other consequences of a potential amnesty.

1. When Do We Give Amnesty?

To help focus our thoughts about tax amnesties, we believe it is useful to consider the justifications for other kinds of amnesty. When have societies given amnesties? What characteristics do amnesties share? What purposes are they alleged to serve, and what do they actually accomplish? When are they socially productive? Having explored these issues, we shall return to the special case of tax amnesties.

Amnesties are not unusual. In the past two decades, governments in the United States have given amnesties for draft evasion, parking tickets, unreturned library books, and now tax evasion. Perhaps the most significant amnesty was signed into law this fall; it offers permanent residence status to an estimated 4 million illegal aliens who entered the United States before January 1982. In conjunction with the amnesty, substantial penalties will be imposed on employers of ineligible and future illegal aliens, with a promised increase in enforcement efforts. This amnesty eases the transition to a new regime, in part by exempting old offenders, whose sheer numbers would make strict enforcement impossible. It also reflects a political compromise between defenders of present illegal residents (amnesty supporters) and the interests seeking to stem the illegal tide, who gain significant sanctions for new offenses.

It is common, though not universal, for the winners of a war to provide some form of amnesty for those who honestly supported and honorably defended the losing side. Many societies give continuing amnesties for some offenses. Statutes of limitations erase liability for torts and for prosecution for misdemeanors and most felonies (but not federal tax fraud!); large library fines are often imposed but seem almost never to be collected. Some amnesties are formal and require an application process and documentation; others are unadvertised.[1] For example, most revenue collectors waive some penalties for taxpayers who claim administrative error as a cause of their noncompliance with tax laws and who voluntarily appear to pay the tax and any interest due.

Other social conventions akin to amnesty are also common. The enforcement of some laws is so casual as to constitute a practical amnesty. Drivers in large packs of automobiles traveling a few miles per hour over the speed limit are virtually immune from speeding tickets; citizens are so unlikely to be penalized for keeping small amounts of marijuana for private use in their homes that society might as well have declared an amnesty; ancient laws about sexual practices are routinely ignored and largely unenforced. Lax enforcement sometimes reflects simple priority setting. Some laws are viewed as obsolete, given changing social norms, and we naturally direct scarce enforcement resources toward more important offenses. But other choices are unrelated to the seriousness of the crimes. Low-level street crime in some communities enjoys something like continuing amnesty because jails are overcrowded; enforcement authorities, aware that penalties are being waived for most convictions, direct their attention and arrests toward offenders who can successfully compete for space in jail.

For many violations, however, societies never give amnesties and virtually never even give pardons. For heinous crimes, major frauds like embezzlement, or desertion from a combat unit under fire, no serious consideration is given to blanket abatements of penalties (though in carefully reviewed cases with extenuating circumstances, an individual offender may be shown leniency).

In what circumstances are amnesties particularly likely? First, societies generally give amnesties for offenses committed by a relatively

---

1. In Biblical times, some were even regularly scheduled. The Old Testament refers to jubilee years, at half-century intervals, in which debtor slaves were to be freed and "alienated property" was to be returned to its rightful owner. See Leviticus 25:8–34.

large number of otherwise reasonably ordinary citizens, whose allegiance and noncriminal reputations we wish to maintain or reclaim. A classic example is draft evasion in a war that is unpopular or widely perceived as unjust. Many young men evaded the draft in the Vietnam era. Though by no means a random sample of draft-age citizens, they were not significantly set apart from other citizens *except as a result of evading the draft*. Similarly, people with many parking tickets are difficult to distinguish from the rest of us.[2] When a law is sufficiently flouted, it becomes illegitimate. In some cases, we modify the law. But when, as with taxes and illegal aliens, changing the law is particularly undesirable—we need government revenues, and we will not throw open our doors to immigrants—amnesty may provide a way to recapture legitimacy.

Second, societies are more likely to give amnesties for an offense that did not directly damage an *identified* party. Contrast draft evasion with desertion under fire. Draft evasion certainly affects other people—someone else will be forced to serve—but it is hard to know exactly whom.[3] Desertion from a combat unit under fire, in sharp contrast, directly endangers the lives of an identified group of individuals and is therefore harder to forgive.

Third, we are more likely to declare an amnesty for a violation that is unrelated to other offenses. Society is more likely to provide amnesty for private home use of small amounts of marijuana than for assault, theft, or burglary. Smoking marijuana at home, at least under current social mores, is not a very strong indication of sociopathic behavior. Being in-

2. In some cases (parking tickets and library fines may be examples) our inability to enforce rules has led to undesirable equilibrium involving little compliance, little revenue, and many offenders outside the social contract. Better enforcement technology (for example, computerized recordkeeping or the Denver Boot) may improve the ongoing equilibrium, reducing the need for amnesties.
3. One suspects, however, that those with draft lottery numbers just ahead of the cutoff, who would have escaped being drafted had there been fewer evaders, might have been more likely than others to oppose the draft evasion amnesty.

Box 1 AMNESTIES ARE MORE LIKELY WHEN

• Many otherwise ordinary citizens participated in illicit activity.
• The offense did not directly harm identified individuals.
• The offense is not chronic or linked to a pattern of other offenses.
• Enforcement will be nearly impossible anyway.

volved in street crime is more strongly linked to a pattern society wants to discourage.

Fourth, amnesties seem to be more likely when society will find it difficult to enforce the penalty anyway. Forgiving library fines is a good way to recover books, particularly when the alternative is to have neither the books nor the fines. Proponents of amnesty for illegal aliens argue that it would be too costly and too painful to find and deport the multitude who established residence in the United States some years ago, and that society might as well declare this reality to be in conformance with the law. Society gains by eliminating the deadweight loss (of books not available at the library and of residents who must avoid contact with public agencies) and by bringing the violators into conformance with social norms when there is little to gain by keeping them estranged.

2. Benefits and Costs of Amnesties

What do societies seek to gain by offering amnesties? Commonly, there are seven main benefits. First, an amnesty may enable us to collect some proportion of past debts that otherwise would be uncollectable. In 1983, for example, Philadelphia collected over 160,000 volumes during its highly publicized one-week library amnesty—books that would otherwise have been lost to its system. (That event apparently provoked much mutual congratulation and removed a load of guilt from 35,000 patrons, whom the library praised as showing "great respect for reading and libraries.") Parking and tax amnesties do not eliminate the original charges, just the supplementary penalties. In effect, delinquents are offered a chance to clear the slate by paying some of what they owe. Illegal aliens eligible for permanent residence under our new legislation will be allowed eighteen months to get on the books, become taxpayers, and so on. Failing this, they will be liable to expulsion.

Second, amnesties encourage renewed compliance. After a parking amnesty, people may take more care to park legally. This benefit is particularly large when, in the absence of an amnesty, there is a strong incentive for delinquents to remain so. A draft evader who wanted to return from Canada and go straight in 1972 no longer faced Vietnam but Leavenworth. Tax evaders, to hide past delinquency, often must continue to cheat. A bank cannot advance further credit to a corporation (or country) in default, even if the new loan is expected to be profitable.[4]

4. It is often difficult to distinguish profitable and realistically refinanced loans from refinancing designed to conceal bad debts. The Small Business Administration has often been accused of using rollovers to keep down the reported rate of default, and some of

Amnesties allow society to rearrange incentives that otherwise favor continued noncompliance on the part of a delinquent.

Third, giving an amnesty often makes the society better able to control the future. The conquering army that offers amnesty to its vanquished opponents if they surrender their arms—and threatens powerful action against those who do not cooperate by a given date—not only begins to heal society's wounds but dramatically reduces the potential for future armed conflict. (The military analogy seems appropriate in judging the tax amnesty of our home state of Massachusetts.) Parking ticket amnesties result in a current address list useful in future collection efforts, thus making future compliance more likely. An amnesty for toxic waste dumps might permit society to find out where they are before poisons filter into groundwater. And a tax amnesty makes future adherence to the tax code more likely by removing the need to conceal past sins. An amnesty is desirable if it lowers the cost of behaving well in the future.

Fourth, amnesties allow society to forgive violators who are unlikely to become repeat offenders, penitents, individuals who have become delinquent by blunder, or offenders who have transgressed some rule society regards as minor. Some violations may have sprung from well-intentioned behavior. For example, many of those who evaded the Vietnam draft did so out of honest disagreement with their government; they can claim a loyalty to principles that society strongly supports. Although society cannot affirm their decision to evade, it may want to mitigate the penalty; amnesty after the war provides one avenue.

Fifth, amnesties help to reduce or eliminate deadweight burdens from a social schism or from individual guilt. The threat of punishment may deter an offense, but once deterrence has failed, the continuing guilt or ostracism serves little purpose. Punishment may deter future offenses, but it cannot change what is already done. Once the desire for retribution or revenge has been long enough served, the time may come to bury the hatchet to reduce the implied waste.

Sixth, amnesties may permit society to declare that it made a mistake and now wants to change its mind. Some believe that the Vietnam draft amnesty is at least ambiguous in this respect and, therefore, perhaps particularly dangerous. Establishing that society can change its mind may make many kinds of socially undesirable behavior more attractive

the arrangements offering new credit to developing countries that are overextended appear to be of this form. An official amnesty may provide a way to terminate such undesirable behavior. Indeed, amnesties that will officially waive or reduce some debt repayment by developing countries have been widely discussed, because it seems likely that full-value repayments will never be made.

and undercut social norms. Some observers might interpret an amnesty for past marijuana offenses as a sign that an amnesty for cocaine will eventually be offered.[5]

Finally, amnesties can make the transition to a new enforcement regime seem more fair. When society systematically fails to enforce a law over a long period, it implicitly creates a presumption that the offense is not serious, encouraging otherwise honorable members of society to choose noncompliance. Surveys suggest that as many as one third of Americans think that tax cheating can be condoned. Under such circumstances, it may seem unfair to change the degree of enforcement, subjecting those who offended under a known lax enforcement regime to penalties consistent with a harsher view of the offense.[6]

Even for offenses regarded as serious, a longstanding failure to identify and punish perpetrators may reduce the legitimacy of a later roundup. As we debate how to improve enforcement of immigration laws—sending the message that illegal residence (or employing illegal aliens) is a serious offense—we also consider amnesty for those who have been in residence long enough. After so many years of ineffective action, it seems unfair to enforce the law on those individuals now. Due process requires fair warning.[7] And for those who object that amnesty reduces the legitimacy of the original system, the promise of stricter enforcement in the future may be an adequate compensation. Both softies and disciplinarians may prefer a system with reduced penalties now and stiffer penalties later to the status quo.

5. Indeed, some people oppose a tax amnesty because it would seem to make evasion less of a crime. No doubt such thinking underlies the nearly universal agreement that any tax amnesty would have to be backed by a much more rigorous enforcement effort. Whereas the immigration amnesty is expected to decrease the scale of the enforcement problem dramatically, no one expects tax amnesties to reduce evasion enough to permit a substantial relaxation of enforcement. More enforcement in the tax area will simply require more resources devoted to this task.

6. The seemingly accidental and arbitrary enforcement of the Georgia law prohibiting sodomy, recently affirmed by the Supreme Court, struck many observers this way. The Court affirmed the state's right to prohibit sexual behavior it regards as illicit even if conducted by consenting adults in their homes, but it did not comment on the differential enforcement issue. That is, no one raised the issue of the constitutionality of enforcing a law that is generally so casually enforced that apprehension would almost necessarily be accidental.

7. Both privately and publicly, we generally avoid the apparent unfairness that comes from changing our implicit contracts about enforcement. As our children grow older and more responsible, we do not enforce rules retroactively even if they were aware of them. We declare that prior violations are exempt (amnestied), but that in the future punishment will be consistent and more severe. The principle of not subjecting people to punishment more severe than what they can reasonably be said to have risked when they commited the offense is embodied in our norms for parental behavior, our common law, and our constitutional prohibition against ex post facto laws.

Amnesties clearly have costs as well as benefits. First, they often annoy nondelinquents. One of the authors usually obeys speed limits and thinks speeders should be ticketed; the other would like to drive faster and feels like a chump because those who are driving faster are not being arrested. Neither of us particularly likes the quasi amnesty we observe.

Second, amnesties may have undesirable incentive effects. Will those subject to the next military conscription remember that Vietnam draft evaders were eventually given amnesty? Will that knowledge inappropriately tilt their choices in a socially undesirable direction? Why pay parking tickets now if there will be an amnesty later? Why return any library book now if you can keep it free until the next amnesty?

To minimize these incentive effects, officials declare many amnesties to be on a "one-time-only" basis. If an amnesty is believed to be truly unique, it affects only past actions, which cannot be changed, and should have no impact on future decisions. But it may be hard to make a firm commitment never to have another amnesty. If it made sense once, why will it not make sense again? Moreover, many amnesties are clearly foreseeable. The United States has given amnesties for draft evasion after each war; library amnesties are given regularly.[8] In these instances, the bad incentive effects of an amnesty were evidently thought to be outweighed by the benefits of drawing society back together.[9]

Amnesties have another potentially critical disadvantage: they undermine the strength of the social sanction against the amnestied behavior, reducing the guilt felt by delinquents when they misbehave. Guilt, or its cousin shame, is a highly efficient tool for social control. It is imposed automatically, with certainty, for any misbehavior by anyone with a conscience. And it works. Most people have many chances to steal with virtually no chance of being caught, yet few do so. Societies therefore expend great effort to instill the values that create conscience.

Even vigorous enforcement efforts can detect only a small fraction of offenders. If we must rely on citizens' desire to avoid imposed penalties (rather than shared values) to ensure compliance with the law, penalties must be large enough to balance out the low probability of apprehension. In fact, we may be reluctant actually to impose such severe punishment.[10]

8. Other amnesties are also predictable. No victorious army in modern times has sought permanently to enslave the defeated population (though that was a common practice for thousands of years). In this instance, of course, the incentive effect operates in the opposite direction. Knowing that it will not be enslaved, the enemy may not fight so hard.
9. The fact that amnesties yield present benefits and future costs sets up a political incentive structure that may produce too many amnesties, as administrations with limited lifespans hasten to collect the benefits while leaving many of the costs to their successors.
10. Western justice, perhaps still in the (no more than an) eye-for-an-eye tradition, has

As guilt—or, to put it positively, the warm feeling that comes from being diligent and honest—diminishes as a force in the compliance decision, society must rely on the considerably more expensive and less efficient approach of identifying and punishing delinquents—both tasks that must be conducted under strict rules protecting citizens' (and convicts') rights. If amnesties significantly reduce the guilt associated with future noncompliance, they may be a bad bargain indeed.[11]

3. Benefits and Costs of Tax Amnesties

In several respects, tax evasion is the kind of offense for which amnesty is relatively likely, or at least plausible. No doubt some people became tax delinquents by mistake and would now like to become honest citizens but are deterred by the expense or embarrassment. A significant proportion of taxes is evaded, nearly 20 percent at the federal level, it is estimated. Tax evasion by one person does not directly harm other identifiable individuals. Most past tax evasion will be difficult to detect if it has not already been identified, so a tax amnesty is making official what is highly probable anyway.

Moreover, tax amnesties may provide the benefits often sought from amnesties in other areas. They reduce guilt of evaders (many of them otherwise ordinary citizens), a deadweight loss that hurts them without helping anyone else. They provide direct benefits in the form of voluntary back tax payments. They help to reduce future noncompliance by adding former delinquents to the tax rolls and removing the danger that past malfeasance will be revealed. And, perhaps most important, amnesties smooth the transition to a new, harsher regime of tax law enforcement with fair warning.

But tax amnesties may also share the disadvantages of other amnesty programs. Ordinary citizens who have been paying their taxes may feel

---

rarely incorporated probability of detection as a significant factor in setting penalties. Partly for this reason, no doubt, penalties for tax noncompliance are quite low. The charge for late payment is 5 percent of tax due per month up to a maximum of 25 percent. The penalty for negligence is only an additional 5 percent of the tax due. Clearly our present scale of penalties is not designed for our present situation, where the probability of an audit is less than 1 percent, and even then an offense may not be provable or even identified.

11. Undoubtedly there are even what economists call externalities—guilt and legitimacy effects felt beyond the specific arena of the amnesty. Indeed, this may be a critical argument against an amnesty for past toxic waste dumping, despite the health gains it might offer by making future dumping less likely. The legitimacy of all society's rules would be diminished if we announced that people who have risked the public health may get off scot-free. Similarly, when we excuse past tax evaders, violators of all laws look a little less disreputable, though the externality would seem to be less severe.

unjustly treated either because they are denied vengeance or because they are made to feel like chumps. Moreover, depending on the form of amnesty granted and the perceived likelihood of repetition, tax amnesties might encourage evasion, allowing delinquents to hope they may later be able to reconsider freely.

Many amnesties relate to single or sporadic offenses, such as a student occupation of a college building, the possession of handguns when they are declared illegal, or draft evasion during the Vietnam War. Our tax program, by contrast, will continue indefinitely, and chiselers and cheaters will always be among us. In this respect, tax amnesties resemble programs offering permanent residence status for long-time illegal aliens or parking ticket amnesties. The amnesty must be viewed in terms of long-term objectives of securing future compliance—for example, deterring new illegal aliens by making them unemployable. That is why tax amnesties, and our nation's new immigration amnesty, are linked with stiff enforcement programs for the future. We are trying not only to bring past violators back into the fold as full-fledged citizens (a principal objective of the Vietnam draft amnesty) but also to prevent strays in the future.

Finally, and perhaps most importantly, amnesty for tax evasion may make cheating seem less significant, reducing the guilt felt by those who consider stretching their deductions or underreporting their income. A substantial fraction of taxpayers may behave honestly because they (probably incorrectly) believe cheating is likely to be detected, but many others probably comply because they believe it is the right thing to do.[12] If amnesties make evasion seem forgivable and thus insignificant, they may have serious financial consequences in reducing voluntary compliance over the long run. In addition to equity losses, this will mean higher and, therefore, less efficient tax rates.

The continuing nature of our tax collection system is a critical feature distinguishing tax amnesty from, for example, a draft-evaders amnesty for a particular war (which merely reduces penalties). A tax amnesty is almost inevitably coupled with increased penalties and enforcement efforts. The penalty schedule is twisted, not necessarily lowered. If strong sanctions are prerequisites for maintenance of guilt and conscience (and possible ostracism for offenders), then a tax amnesty could actually be part of a guilt-*strengthening* effort.

---

12. We want tax evasion to have the moral connotation of stealing in contrast to offenses like illegal parking, for which hardly anyone suffers pangs of conscience. (A decision not to feed the meter seems merely a small wager with the parking department, of no consequence beyond the money involved).

Box 2 ADVANTAGES AND DISADVANTAGES OF TAX AMNESTY/
ENFORCEMENT PACKAGE

Major potential advantages	Likely importance of actual effects
• Collects back taxes	Important
• Increases future compliance by lowering its cost (no longer necessary to evade to hide past bad behavior)	Important
• Improves records, e.g., adding nonfilers, which enhances future control of evasion	Important
• Reduces deadweight costs from burden of guilt; fosters repentance	Potentially important, but not a salient political argument
• Permits politically feasible transition to harsher enforcement regime	Very important
—Lowers short-term penalties, raises long-term; such twisting can raise or lower on net	Important in forging political compromise between soft hearts and disciplinarians
—Avoids "inequity" from sudden change	Limited importance given lack of political constituency supporting tax evasion
—Permits imposition of severe penalties on those who refuse amnesty offer	Important
—Permits productive and vigorous enforcement against future evasion	Very important
• Angers honest taxpayers	Important
• Undermines guilt from tax evasion	Does not apply if amnesty is combined with substantial strengthening of enforcement, harsher penalties, etc.
• Reduces fear of future sanctions that may be amnestied	Only relevant if managed poorly

4. Tax Amnesty in Practice: The Massachusetts Experience

Nineteen states have conducted explicit tax amnesties in the last three years, collecting about $1 billion in what they consider otherwise largely uncollectible taxes from over 500,000 taxpayers. Three states are currently in the midst of amnesty periods; two others have legislative authorization to begin amnesties soon. The programs have generally involved forgiveness of criminal and civil penalties for those who came forward to declare their delinquency and pay the tax they owed, together with a (possibly substantial) interest charge for the "loan" they had obtained by not paying earlier. Those whom the state has already informed of a suspected delinquency are often excluded or given only partial amnesty.

The highly publicized Massachusetts program, which became something of an archetype, ran from October 17, 1983, to January 17, 1984. Its avowed purpose was to collect revenue immediately, to permit transition to a new regime of considerably tougher enforcement, and to increase voluntary compliance in the future by getting current delinquents onto the tax rolls and encouraging them to stay there. The program was, on its own terms, wildly successful. Even the most optimistic forecasters within the Department of Revenue had guessed that the immediate payments from amnestied taxpayers would not exceed $20 million. When the dust settled and the 52,000 amnesty applications were tallied, the state had collected $85 million, at a cost of only $2 million for extra staff and other direct program expenditures. Amnesty payments were received for every major tax the state imposes, though delinquencies related to personal and corporate income taxes generated well over half of the payments. Over 60 percent of the payments were from taxpayers who had not previously filed any information about the tax they came forward to pay. Among income tax delinquents, about half of the delinquencies were for a single year, but over 20 percent were for four years or more.

The Massachusetts amnesty was combined with a heightened emphasis on enforcement. The amnesty period was preceded by a series of dramatic enforcement actions, including highly publicized seizures of assets from taxpayers the state claimed were delinquent. New legislation (which included the authorization for amnesty) had recently stiffened the penalties for evasion, permitted felony prosecution for some particularly flagrant evaders, allowed the Commonwealth to revoke the licenses of or cancel contracts with delinquents, and provided additional staff and enforcement resources (including new funds for computers to track delinquents more reliably).

In this context, which presumably heightened the anxiety of delinquents, the temporary amnesty period, announced with only one day of public warning, was presented as a never-to-be-repeated chance to get on the right side of the law. The enforcement agencies had been displaying their new, sharper teeth. Many Massachusetts tax delinquents probably had believed that the Commonwealth would never get serious about tracking them down and collecting unpaid taxes and penalties. Now suddenly things looked different. Assets were seized, restaurants closed, hotels shut down. Tax evaders faced felony prosecution, and it seemed as if some would actually go to jail. A surprising number of delinquents seized the opportunity offered by amnesty to pay up and stop worrying about how much bite might be behind the bark.

But the direct payments made under the amnesty program were only one class of benefit. The program also played an important role helping Massachusetts move to a new period of stiffer enforcement without seeming to break an implicit contract with taxpayers about how much enforcement scrutiny there would be. Since concentrating the new enforcement resources on prior delinquents was likely to be procedurally difficult and conceivably to appear unjust, and since only a small percentage of past delinquents was likely to be discovered, there was little reason to try to clear out the inventory of delinquents through direct enforcement. Why not declare an amnesty and let them pay up on their own, particularly since this approach would probably yield more money?[13] An individual who failed to come forward despite the amnesty program would then seem fairer game for a stern penalty program. Using an amnesty to smooth the rough edge of the transition also struck a useful political compromise between self-avowed softies and hardliners.

The new enforcement regime is expected to have two major benefits: (1) the state may be able to increase its collections from future delinquents substantially; (2) future voluntary compliance with the tax code may be increased. Massachusetts has estimated both of these effects and claims they are large in comparison with the direct returns of amnesty. According to Department of Revenue figures, audit assessments pur-

---

13. In theory, individuals would multiply what they owe if caught by the probability of getting caught and choose amnesty only if they save money on average. But several kinds of conditions will make an amnesty in conjunction with a bolstered enforcement effort likely to collect more revenues than the enforcement effort alone: (1) Individuals miscalculate or fail to calculate; the publicity accompanying the amnesty may encourage them to participate. (2) Individuals are risk averse on the magnitude of fines. (3) There are nonconservative penalties such as shame or jail. (4) Amnesty allows for legitimate repentance and an escape from unfavorable self-perception. (5) Amnesty induces enough discoverable delinquents to come forward that the population of remaining delinquents is reduced and their probability of discovery is increased. (6) Those who participate in an amnesty may provide information that implicates other evaders, thus changing the probability of detection.

suant to the new enforcement efforts in fiscal years (FY) 1983 through 1985 exceeded those of the prior three-year period by $263 million. Total collections of delinquent taxes (excluding receipts under amnesty) were up $130 million over the same period. And, from a comparison of econometric estimates of tax revenues (based on preamnesty behavior) with actual collections in FY 1984 and 1985, the Commonwealth estimates that improvements in voluntary compliance have resulted in $480 million in extra tax payments across the two-year period (excluding the direct collections from amnesty).[14]

Since it is impossible to know exactly what level of tax payments would have prevailed in the absence of tougher enforcement and amnesty, these estimates must be viewed with caution. They do suggest, however, that the continuing payoffs from more vigorous enforcement— greater delinquent tax collection and more voluntary compliance— substantially exceed the direct revenues from the amnesty.

A few figures will put the gains from amnesty in perspective. Massachusetts' revenues in FY 1984 were $5.8 billion. Direct amnesty revenues (from an expressly one-time initiative) were $85 million, or 1.5 percent of annual revenues. A generous estimate would put the measurable impact of the amnesty and enforcement program at roughly $400 million per year, or about a 6 percent increase in annual revenues. If there is greater voluntary compliance now, there will be less delinquent tax to find and assess later, which suggests that straight extrapolations based on short-term state experiences would be generous indeed. But even if we cut these figures by two thirds and consider a 2 percent increase in the permanent level of annual revenues, the impact is still far more important than a one-time collection of 1 or 2 percent of revenues. The revenue effectiveness of an amnesty and enforcement initiative depends primarily on the extent to which it shifts collections permanently upward, not how much it yields on a one-time basis.

5. The Effects of State Tax Amnesties

The roots of state tax amnesty programs are obscure. Illinois sponsored a small program in 1982, raising less than $100,000 in amnesty collections. Large-scale programs began in 1983, when four states ran official tax amnesty programs. Of these, only Arizona collected more than $1 million or more than 0.05 percent of state tax revenues; its collections were nearly 0.3 percent of state tax revenues for the year. Seven states fielded

---

14. Such massive gains may not be repeated. Given higher voluntary compliance, presumably the backlog of assessable delinquent taxes will shrink in the future.

programs in 1984–programs straddling year-end are classified under their concluding year—collecting over $250 million in total, with two states (Massachusetts and Illinois) collecting 1.5 percent or more of state tax collections in that year through amnesty payments. The following year saw a large program in California, which raised nearly $150 million, about 0.5 percent of tax revenue. Several smaller states had moderate-sized amnesty programs. There has been strong continuing interest in 1986, with New York collecting $360 million and Michigan $103 million (about 1.7 percent and 1.1 percent of annual revenues, respectively).

Table 1   TAX AMNESTY COLLECTIONS IN DOLLARS AND AS A PERCENTAGE OF STATE TAX REVENUES, 1982–1986

	Direct amnesty collections	
Year and state	Dollars (millions)	State taxes (%)
1982 Amnesties		
Illinois	0.1	—
1983 Amnesties		
Arizona	6.0	0.3
Idaho	0.3	—
Missouri	0.9	—
North Dakota	0.2	—
1984 Amnesties		
Alabama	3.2	0.1
Illinois	152.4	1.8
Kansas	0.6	—
Massachusetts	84.5	1.5
Minnesota	11.9	0.2
Oklahoma	13.9	0.5
Texas	0.5	—
1985 Amnesties		
California	146.5	0.5
Colorado	6.0	0.3
Louisiana	1.2	—
New Mexico	13.9	1.0
South Carolina	7.1	0.2
Wisconsin	20.0	0.4
1986 Amnesties		
Michigan	102.5	1.1
New York	363.2	1.7

—indicates < 0.05.
Source: Summary figures from Massachusetts Department of Revenue; individual state departments of revenue for their own figures; *Business Week*, March 10, 1986, p. 31. All 1986 values are estimates.

Table 1 summarizes the states' experience, showing the level of direct tax amnesty collections both in dollars and as a fraction of state tax revenues.

Have amnesty programs affected compliance? Any analysis must deal with worlds that never existed, since there is no control group of states that have significantly bolstered enforcement without offering amnesty, or offered amnesties without an increase in stringency. Thus we have no way to know whether the Massachusetts program of tougher enforcement would have been socially palatable and politically feasible, and worked equally as well, in the absence of an amnesty. We can, however, observe the growth of state tax revenues in states with and without amnesties. Table 2 shows the difference between the annual growth rate of tax revenues in states with tax amnesties in 1984 and 1985 and in states that had no tax amnesty. As the first column indicates, tax revenues grew more slowly from 1980 to 1983 in states that later had tax amnesties than in states that did not.[15] If all states that had tax amnesties in 1984 and 1985 are included, their tax revenues grew about one percentage point slower than other states in the period from 1980 to 1983. But from 1983 to 1985, when we would expect to see the effects of their tax amnesties, these states' revenues grew faster than those of the other states, by approximately one-half percentage point. Thus, relative to states without amnesties, the annual growth rate of tax revenues in amnesty states shifted up by about one and one-half percentage points during the pe-

15. The slower growth of revenues in these states may have created particularly severe pressure to find new revenues or improve their tax compliance.

Table 2 DIFFERENCES IN ANNUAL GROWTH RATES OF TAX REVENUES BETWEEN STATES WITH TAX AMNESTIES IN 1984 AND 1985 AND THOSE WITHOUT TAX AMNESTY, 1980–1985

Amnesties	1980–1983	1983–1985	Shift
All	−1.03	+0.50	+1.53
Collections > 0.3% of revenues	−2.90	+0.67	+3.57
Collections > 0.5% of revenues	−3.27	+1.25	+4.52
Collections > 1.0% of revenues	−3.44	+0.31	+3.73

Figures in first two columns show difference between annual growth rate in tax revenues in states that had amnesties in 1984 or 1985 and annual growth rate in tax revenues in states that had no amnesty. Figures in third column show shift in growth rate of tax revenues in amnesty as compared to nonamnesty states between early period (1980–1983) and later period (1983–1985).

Source: Table 1 and U.S. Bureau of the Census, State tax collections, various years.

riod in which the amnesties operated. (If the amnesty monies were non-recurring, states running successful amnesties in 1984 would show no exceptional increase in growth rates from 1983 to 1985.)

These results become stronger if we focus on states with particularly large tax amnesty programs. As Table 2 indicates, in states with amnesties collecting over 0.3 percent of state tax revenues, the annual growth rate of tax revenues shifted up by 3.5 percentage points as compared with nonamnesty states during the period of the amnesties, with slightly larger shifts if the threshold is raised to 0.5 percent or to 1 percent of tax revenues.

Looking solely at states with amnesties in 1984 provides some evidence that the revenue growth effect persists beyond the year in which amnesty operates. Table 3 shows the tax revenue growth rates between 1982 and 1985 for 1984 amnesty states; for the subset of 1984 amnesty states with amnesty collections of more than 0.3 percent of 1984 tax revenue; and for other states. In the period before amnesty took effect (1982 to 1983), tax revenues in the 1984 amnesty states grew more slowly than in other states, by three to four percentage points. During the actual operation of the amnesty (1983 to 1984), their revenues grew at a rate closer to that of the other states, but still about two percentage points lower. During the postamnesty period (1984 to 1985), their revenues grew faster than in other states by one to two percentage points. The shift is more dramatic for states with larger tax amnesties (as measured by the fraction of state tax revenues collected through amnesty payments), presumably because of greater earlier noncompliance or more vigorous gains in enforcement. These results are only suggestive, particularly because fiscal years and calendar years do not match in most states, and in some cases amnesty revenue may be split across two tax

Table 3   ANNUAL TAX REVENUE GROWTH RATES FOR 1984 TAX AMNESTY STATES AND OTHER STATES, 1982–1985 (PERCENT)

	1982–1983	1983–1984	1984–1985
Amnesty states			
All 1984 tax amnesty states	2.9	13.1	10.4
1984 tax amnesty states with amnesty collections > 0.3% of tax revenues	1.8	13.1	9.5
Nonamnesty states			
Other states	6.0	15.3	8.8

Source: Table 1 and U.S. Bureau of the Census, *State tax collections,* various years.

years. Nevertheless, these figures suggest that the revenue growth associated with amnesty and its accompanying enforcement persists beyond the period in which amnesty is declared.

There are many differences between the economies and tax systems of amnesty and nonamnesty states, which may explain some of the observed shift in tax revenue growth rates. These results must therefore be viewed with caution. Still, it is striking that in the period before they declared their amnesties, the tax revenues of amnesty states were growing more slowly than the national average; after tax amnesty, their revenues grew faster than the national average. If amnesty, with an associated greater enforcement effort, is not the explanation, it is at least strongly correlated with whatever the deeper explanation might be. For states that later had amnesty collections of over 0.3 percent of tax revenues, annual growth in tax revenues in the period before amnesty was about two thirds of the national average; after amnesty, it was slightly above the national average. (Background figures for these calculations are not presented in the tables.) This is quite a substantial shift; even if it does not persist beyond these two years, it would lift tax revenues in these states by 2 to 10 percent above what would have been expected on the basis of the preamnesty period.

How much additional revenue flowed from these states' amnesty and enforcement programs? To provide a crude measure, we projected what tax revenues in 1984 and 1985 amnesty states might have been in the absence of amnesties if the difference from the national average in their revenue growth rates before amnesty had persisted in 1984 and 1985.[16] Although the projections for each state are subject to considerable variation, the aggregate estimates provide a speculative basis for assessing the total revenue gain associated with tax amnesty programs.

Using this approach, we estimate aggregate gains between $3 billion and $5 billion from 1984 to 1985 in the tax amnesty states.[17] Their actual

16. Proceeding state by state, we first measured the difference between each state's growth in revenues and the national average growth for the preamnesty period. Using 1983 observed revenues, we then projected 1984 revenues in the absence of amnesty by assuming that the state's revenue growth rate would have continued to differ from the national average by the same amount as in the preamnesty period. We then compared the estimated revenues without amnesty to the revenues actually observed with the amnesty programs in place. This amounts to fitting a fixed-effects model for state revenue growth rates, with each state permitted to have growth differing from the national average and to have its own "amnesty" effect. In particular, it assumes no regression toward the mean. We place little reliance on the individual state results, preferring instead to examine the aggregated results.

17. We obtain a range of estimates because there are various plausible ways to estimate revenues in the amnesty states under the hypothetical scenario "without amnesty." Using different base periods to measure state differentials from the national average,

revenues in that period were about $120 billion, so the extra revenues apparently associated with their amnesty programs are about 3 to 5 percent of the revenues collected.[18]

6. Toward a Federal Tax Amnesty Revenue Estimate

The apparent success of state tax amnesty programs, together with historic federal budget deficits, has prompted a variety of proposals for a tax amnesty program at the federal level. Governors of states with successful experiences have pushed the idea. It has been proposed in various forms in Congress. The president has expressed interest. The commissioner of the Internal Revenue Service (IRS) has adamantly resisted suggestions to pursue the idea, but proponents press on. The sweeping tax reform package, recently signed into law, represents a change in regimes that provides a perfect occasion for amnesty, and its phasing provides a rather broad window of opportunity. A program combining amnesty and stricter subsequent enforcement would be expected to increase voluntary tax compliance. Deficits would be reduced, not by forcibly taxing away hard-earned dollars from reluctant taxpayers, but through voluntary contributions from taxpayers happy to have an opportunity to come clean and go straight. So argue the proponents of a federal tax amnesty.

Can the state experience help us understand what might happen under a federal amnesty? There are difficult hurdles to overcome in applying lessons from the state to the federal level. Knowledgeable commentators have taken several tacks. Allen Lerman of Treasury's Office of Tax Analysis has argued that analysis should be limited to amnesty by itself, not amnesty in conjunction with an increase in enforcement effort.[19] There are two reasons to adopt this focus. First, it is a relevant question in itself—we may well wish to know the independent effect of amnesty, not just the effect of amnesty combined with additional enforcement effort, because we can (and do) operate the two policies sepa-

---

projecting 1985 revenues one year forward from 1984 rather than two years forward from 1983, and other small changes in assumptions result in minor variations in the results. We are certain that other approaches to making these projections would lead to different results and that alternative explanations having nothing to do with amnesty could be advanced. Nonetheless, our results do not seem implausible, and they are robust against small variations in the assumptions underlying the calculations presented here.

18. This counts revenues and tax amnesty gains for 1984 for the 1984 amnesty states only; revenues and gains for 1985 are counted for both 1984 and 1985 amnesty states.

19. Allen H. Lerman, Tax amnesty: The federal perspective. *National Tax Journal* 39, no. 3 (1986):325–32.

rately. Second, we may regard the federal enforcement effort as already adequate or, in any case, unlikely to be changed. If so, we again want to focus on amnesty by itself.

Lerman estimates that the one-time revenue gains from federal amnesty per se, net of costs and net of revenues actually captured by enforcement efforts rather than amnesty, would be about $1 billion. He takes several different approaches to the estimate, obtaining roughly the same answer each time.

We might, alternatively, try to estimate what a greater enforcement effort would bring in by itself. Many have argued that since federal tax enforcement is better than most states', state amnesty/enforcement packages shed little light on what might be achieved at the federal level. The IRS and analysts at the Office of Management and Budget (OMB) have developed estimates showing how much additional revenue might be collected through enhanced federal enforcement effort.[20] These estimates suggest that both the average and the marginal yield from enforcement spending is dramatically greater than $1 per dollar spent and often greater than $10 per dollar spent. Thus greater enforcement efforts at the federal level should yield substantial revenues. Moreover, these estimates systematically understate the productivity of more enforcement activity, since they exclude the (possibly quite substantial) impact on voluntary compliance. This suggests that there is good reason and ample room for sharpening the tax collector's teeth, even at the federal level.[21] If an amnesty would help us to move to more vigorous enforcement, some proponents would view it as worthwhile for that reason alone.

The results presented above do not permit us to separate the effects of enforcement and of amnesty; indeed, we cannot unequivocally attribute the observed effects to the combination of enforcement and amnesty programs. But, particularly in states with programs that attracted a higher fraction of state tax revenues in amnesty payments, the combined enforcement and amnesty activities tended to be prominent features of the fiscal landscape in the year of amnesty. It seems likely that there is a meaningful relationship between the shifts we observed in state tax revenue growth rates and the launching of dramatic new enforcement efforts

20. See, for example, Frank Malanga, The relationship between IRS enforcement and tax yield. *National Tax Journal* 39, no. 3 (1986):333–37.
21. To maximize net revenues raised, enforcement would be pushed until the last dollar yielded a dollar of revenue, since taxes paid are a transfer, whereas enforcement expenditures represent real resource costs. The efficiency argument for greater enforcement is that it leads to lower overall tax rates, thus reducing adverse consequences for incentives. Many critics, of course, are more interested in the equity effects of enforcement, its ability to distribute more equally the tax burden imposed on individuals with similar incomes.

and tax amnesty programs. And in states with programs perceived as successful, virtually all participants seem to believe that the combination of enhanced enforcement and amnesty worked a special form of magic.

Suppose, then, that we believe (on the basis of IRS and OMB figures) that there is room to enhance federal enforcement and that we do not wish to separate out the independent effect of amnesty; rather, we want to consider how much the federal government might obtain through a combined enforcement/amnesty program. What might the state experience tell us about the prospects for such a program?

The most obvious problem in applying the state experience at the federal level is that the two tax bases have quite different compositions. Many state amnesty programs seem to have been particularly attractive to sales tax delinquents; the virtual absence of excise taxes at the federal level limits the relevance of this part of the state experience. Even if we confine our attention to income taxes, however, state amnesties collected considerable delinquent revenue. Table 4 shows the amnesty collections and the income tax-related portion for the four largest amnesty programs (data on Michigan, the last amnesty program to close, were not available). Amnesty income tax collections as a fraction of annual income tax revenues ranged from just under 1 percent to a bit over 3 percent, with a weighted average of about 2 percent. Since total amnesty collections in these states averaged less than 2 percent of total revenues, income tax collections actually represented a larger proportion of amnesty payments than of tax payments overall.[22] There is no obvious reason to believe that federal revenues are less subject to amnestiable de-

22. This fact is most startling when we consider that virtually all income taxed by the states is taxed by the federal government as well, and that there is a matching program for tax compliance between the two levels.

Table 4   AMNESTY COLLECTIONS AND INCOME TAX–RELATED AMNESTY COLLECTIONS FROM THE FOUR LARGEST TAX AMNESTIES

	Total amnesty collections ($ million)	Income tax amnesty collections ($ million)	Income tax amnesty as fraction of income tax revenues (%)
California	147	103	0.8
Illinois	152	121	3.4
Massachusetts	85	52	1.5
New York	360	209	1.8

Source: Tax Foundation, Inc., Federal tax policy memo, April 1986, p. 3.

linquency than state revenues, at least not by virtue of their composition across taxes.

A second problem is that the state data provide no direct evidence about how many federal tax delinquents would take advantage of an amnesty. There are many ways to cheat on state taxes and still stay within bounds on federal tax impositions. An obvious example is the taxpayer who files federal forms accurately but falsely claims residence in a low-tax state. He or she has much to tell the state tax collector but nothing to confess to a federal tax examiner. Many of the payments collected by state programs were of this general form. Lerman's review of three state amnesties found that well over 90 percent of those who took advantage of the programs had already filed federal forms.[23] By contrast, about 60 percent of those taking advantage of Massachusetts' amnesty had not filed with the state. Only 1 percent were amending previously filed state forms.[24] A second example is people who had already been caught by federal auditors. They knew that the exchange of information between the IRS and state tax collectors would eventually catch up with them; many of them took advantage of the state amnesties as well.

This interaction of federal and state tax codes, enforcement, and evasion cuts in both directions. How shall we interpret the fact that most of the state amnesty filers were already in compliance on their federal taxes? If it indicates that enforcement is much better at the federal level so that taxpayers have cheated more on state than on federal taxes, then a federal amnesty will raise less revenue than the state experience would suggest. However, an alternative interpretation might be that state programs, which were offered without federal participation, were spurned by a large group of noncomplying taxpayers who cheat on *both* federal and state taxes.

Consider the situation of a taxpayer who has failed to report $2000 of income on which he or she would have to pay a 5 percent state tax and a 42 percent federal tax. The state offers an amnesty enabling the delinquent to settle up for a small tax payment (and interest). But it is well known that information on amnesty filers will be made available to the IRS. Thus taking advantage of the state amnesty will result in a much larger tax, interest, and penalty liability at the federal level, with no relief on the penalty part. This cannot have seemed a very attractive bargain. It

23. Lerman, Tax amnesty, n. 3.
24. Massachusetts Department of Revenue, The Massachusetts amnesty program: A statistical synopsis. Mimeo (June 1986). The remaining 39 percent took advantage of amnesty to pay debts already on tax collectors' books as accounts receivable without penalties.

is no wonder that the overwhelming majority of taxpayers who took advantage of the state programs were those already paying their federal taxes (or those coming forward to pay state levies such as sales tax, where there was no accompanying federal charge).

This argument suggests that state programs, however successful, tapped only a portion of the state delinquencies; those that did not also involve a federal delinquency. For this reason, estimating federal amnesty revenue on the basis of state experience systematically underestimates the federal revenue potential. The more that evaded state taxes are associated with evaded federal taxes, the greater the underestimate is likely to be.

Box 3 PROBLEMS IN EXTENDING STATE TAX AMNESTY EXPERIENCE TO FEDERAL LEVEL

- The federal tax base is considerably different from those of states.

  However, one can isolate the significant income tax evasion reported in state amnesties. Net result: problem can be overcome by using data from states on tax bases used by federal government.

- Existing federal enforcement is better than states'.

  IRS and OMB estimates of benefits from additional enforcement spending suggest high returns, though lower than at state level. Net result: experience in states with less aggressive enforcement overstates federal potential.

- Most delinquents claiming state amnesty were in compliance with federal code.

  Appears to suggest that few amnesty takers were not in compliance with federal rules. Also, many were reporting errors and omissions with no federal consequence (for example, reporting income from New Hampshire rather than Massachusetts). The absence of a federal amnesty, however, prevented many in compliance with neither federal nor state tax codes from claiming state amnesty, knowing that the information filed would be made available to the IRS. Net result: state experience probably underestimates federal potential.

Overall Result: Indeterminate, but state experience may well underestimate federal potential.

On net, we suspect, these arguments suggest that the state experience will underestimate the potential of a federal tax amnesty. To be sure, most of those who participated in the state programs were not federal tax delinquents, at least not on these monies. However, federal penalties create strong incentives for federal delinquents not to show up at state amnesty offices. Their absence in the data testifies to their presence of mind.

If extrapolating from the state experience provides an underestimate, then an effective enforcement and amnesty program at the federal level could yield quite substantial revenue. The one-time collection—if greater than 1.5 percent of income tax revenues, as the collections in the four largest state programs were—would be about $10 billion. If the growth in federal revenues responds as state tax revenues apparently have, an additional increase of 1 or 2 percent of annual revenues, and conceivably much more, may be achievable, producing a continuing flow of about $10 billion per year. It is true that we might get much of these increases through stiffened enforcement alone, but without an amnesty a radical change in enforcement procedures seems unlikely.[25]

This estimate of the potential revenue from a combined federal amnesty and enforcement program does not seem unreasonable in light of the amount and composition of federal tax noncompliance. In a widely cited report on tax compliance published in 1983, the IRS estimated that approximately $90 billion in income taxes went unpaid in 1981.[26] As Lerman observes, inflation would raise this total, and the reductions in income tax rates and more effective records matching and other enforcement would reduce it; it seems reasonable to guess that noncompliance is of the same order of magnitude today. A portion of nonpayment—for example, the $9 billion in unpaid taxes on the profits from illegal activity—is unlikely to be susceptible to either amnesty or enforcement (or both). A substantial component, however, estimated at about $70 billion in 1981, is from underreporting income and overstating deductions on submitted tax returns. Some of the large accumulated store of such unacknowledged tax debts might well be susceptible to a well-managed federal amnesty combined with vigorous new enforcement. An additional $3 billion annually is due from tax returns that were never filed. This form of evasion was a particularly fruitful source of payments dur-

25. Indeed, some would argue the trend at the federal level has been in the other direction. The proportion of taxpayers now audited is less than half what it was twenty years ago. The IRS argues that the lower audit rate is more than offset through better targeting, electronic record matching, and other more effective modern information-processing approaches.
26. U.S. Department of Treasury, Internal Revenue Service, *Income tax compliance research: Estimates for 1973–1981*, Washington, D.C., July 1983.

ing state amnesties. Although the federal situation for nonfilers is clearly somewhat different (because federal taxpayers cannot claim that they are filing in another jurisdiction, and therefore that they are not subject to federal taxes), this might still be a source of considerable revenue under a federal amnesty/enforcement package.[27]

Our estimates of the potential revenues cover a wide range; they are subject to considerable doubt. The state experience is difficult to read by itself, and it fits the federal situation only loosely. But if these figures are of the right order of magnitude, they strongly suggest that a combined enforcement and amnesty program at the federal level is well worth careful consideration. They also indicate that a federal program is likely to be more—probably much more—effective if combined with state amnesties.

We argued that the absence of a federal amnesty effectively blocked many taxpayers' access to state amnesty programs, reducing those programs' effectiveness. The problem is less severe in reverse, because state penalties and taxes due are generally much smaller than the federal liability an amnesty filer would voluntarily be accepting. Still, it may be harder to admit "error" when one jurisdiction is forgiving, but another calls you a tax evader (and penalizes you accordingly). There is no obvious reason why states could not be encouraged to facilitate their citizens' access to the federal amnesty by granting a coordinated umbrella amnesty program. (Indeed, Nebraska has already authorized a contingent amnesty program to take effect only in concert with a federal amnesty.) To discourage free-riding states the federal government might conceivably share information about taxpayers filing under the amnesty program only with states that are participating, or might offer amnesty only in conjunction with a state. Citizen ire might well force states to comply. If a few states held out, the program would not be spoiled, though revenues would be reduced.

Just how a federal program would work—whether states would coordinate with it, how many taxpayers might accept the offer, what impact it would have on future compliance—remains in considerable doubt. It seems clear, however, that the upside potential for revenue gains is considerable.[28]

27. Lerman presents a similar argument. Since he concentrates on amnesty alone, however, his analysis answers a different question about the amount of revenue to be gained from underreporting and overdeducting on previously filed forms. He argues that amnesty alone will do little to bring forward those who have consciously evaded their liabilities. Since we are analyzing a combined package of tougher enforcement and amnesty, the $70 billion of "ordinary" tax shaving is a potentially considerable source of revenue. See Lerman, Tax amnesty, pp. 329–31.
28. Several steps could be taken to make amnesties more likely to work. Many forms of tax evasion involve more than one person; society might want to advertise that if you have

7. Explicit Amnesties Within Implicit Amnesties: What Is Really Different?

Society's preference for obtaining confessions rather than convictions generally leads it to offer lower penalties for those who voluntarily admit wrongdoing. There are both moral and strategic reasons for this approach. Thus, an explicit amnesty may be simply a more extreme or better publicized form of a general policy of (partial) forgiveness for the contrite confessed offender. So it is with tax amnesty programs, which generally waive criminal and civil penalties (at least for those who do not already know they are under investigation). But the open secret is that in virtually all jurisdictions criminal penalties and many civil penalties are routinely waived for those who voluntarily disclose and agree to pay tax delinquencies. Except for the most flagrant tax evasions, the outcome of an investigation is some form of confession of error or miscalculation by the delinquent, combined with payment of the back taxes and interest, sometimes including late payment or failure-to-file penalties.

The penalties are low to start with—at the federal level, a maximum of 25 percent of tax liability for late payment and an additional 5 percent for negligence. But even these penalties may be abated in cases with extenuating circumstances, which means in practice that they are sometimes negotiated in return for resolution by agreement rather than through litigation—that is, in return for some form of confession. Both state revenue departments and the IRS abate many of the penalties they assess in the ordinary course of their business; last year the IRS waived nearly 40 percent of the penalties its rules imposed, letting over 4 million taxpayers off the hook for nearly $2 billion in penalties. Since 1978, the IRS has provided abatements to nearly 20 million taxpayers. Commenting on the IRS's practices, Ira Jackson, commissioner of revenue in Massachusetts, observed, "Amnesty merely offers on a wholesale basis what tax partners in big eight accounting firms and every well-informed tax lawyer routinely obtain for their clients on a retail basis."[29]

This assessment, accountants tell us, may somewhat overstate the case. Most penalties are not abated, though some questionable penalties are waived swiftly as part of deals. Nevertheless, the offer of amnesty bears important similarities to what is generally available to delinquents who

---

ever colluded to avoid taxes you had better take advantage of amnesty because your partners might do so, and we will chase down others involved in schemes that come to light under amnesty. Even snitching could be given greater rewards.

29. Ira Jackson, speech to National Tax Association, Tax Institute of America, May 19, 1986, p. 11. Jackson discusses the figures cited above on the frequency with which the IRS abates penalties.

come forth voluntarily. Amnesty differs in four ways: (1) the (relatively small) difference in the terms available, (2) publicity, (3) its importance as an element of a political compromise and as a signaling mechanism fostering a change to a new regime of stricter enforcement, and (4) its inclusion of elements of pardon and redemption.

Which of these features account for the dramatic amnesty collections of the successful states? Surely not the first: a small change in the terms of the deal cannot explain such a sudden influx to the confessional. The second and third factors are related, for amnesties appear to be effective mainly because they are publicized (and therefore draw in many more delinquents) and they permit the curtain to be raised on a new enforcement regime. (The fourth factor is best assessed by psychologists and theologians, not by the economist authors.)

Although any policy of negotiated penalties creates equity problems—some know the penalty structure and others do not, and some have better negotiators—it has the virtue of permitting differentiation among violators. Whatever our reasons for giving amnesty, we are presumably more inclined to give it for some offenses than for others. There is no reason why an amnesty need be a blanket forgiveness, and state programs have generally not been.

Amnesties could be selectively defined. If we want to forgive only small errors, a ceiling can be set. If we think the reporting of some forms of income is more subject to error, and others more to abuse, we may selectively permit amnesty for errors in the types of income less often abused. An amnesty can be selective in the kinds of filers it excuses, the kinds of errors it forgives, the period it covers, and so on. The starting point need not be taxes filed before today; two years from now, the federal government could initiate a selective amnesty that would cover all filings under the "old" tax code but none under the new code. A well-designed selective program could retain much of the benefit of a broader, wholesale clearing of the slate accompanied by stiff penalties for those who do not take advantage of society's "generous offer." An amnesty/enforcement package allows society to ask the repentant sheep to step aside from the incorrigible goats, and it comes with a strong message that the remaining goats will be pursued. Many erstwhile goats may be induced to convert voluntarily to sheephood.

8. Conclusion

Whatever its ultimate effects, an amnesty may seem to represent a relaxation of tax enforcement efforts. Some observers are concerned that such a program would unacceptably undercut the legitimacy of our tax code and of our laws generally. Most citizens seem to pay their taxes primarily as a matter of conscience. If tax amnesties diminish the force of conscience, spreading the message that tax evasion is commonplace and easily forgiven, they may diminish compliance and force society to raise taxes and rely more heavily on less efficient enforcement mechanisms. This is a serious potential liability, which leads to a political prediction: should there be a federal amnesty, it will, like the prominent state amnesties, be linked with a vigorous new enforcement effort. This coupling would reinforce the virtues of strict enforcement. Any punished individuals would have rejected the opportunity to come forth. They could no longer be thought of merely as tax shavers—they would have voluntarily chosen, in the face of a generous offer of reconciliation, to remain tax cheaters.

The loss of conscience should not be a problem in a well-orchestrated enforcement and tax amnesty program. Publicized seizures, arrests, prosecutions, fines, audits, and notices signal that tax evasion has unfortunate consequences, that it is being taken more seriously, that those who do not comply will be an increasingly small and besieged minority. Amnesty is a way out before the trap springs shut. The penalty scale is twisted, not reduced. Evasion is made no less a crime.

An amnesty may provide a socially valuable opportunity to set things straight, to move to a more desirable equilibrium with more widespread honest citizenship and greater punishment of violators—that is, with sharper differentiation between those observing and those outside the social compact.

Though it is conceivable that a strict enforcement program might be

Box 4 POSSIBLE TAX POLICY PROGRAMS

	Current Penalties	Stringent Penalties
No Amnesty	A Status Quo	Raises Penalties B Unlikely Development
Amnesty	Lowers Penalties C Unlikely Development	Lowers Short-Term, Raises Long-Term Penalties D Politically Foreseeable

enacted by itself, the inclusion of an amnesty would offer four advantages. First, merely considering the subject would give the issue new prominence, define it in new terms, get it on the policy agenda, and link it to the tax reform. Second, it might help strike a political balance and foster innovation by making the new outcome appear to be less of a departure from the status quo. Third, the amnesty would represent a way to provide identifiable funds needed for an additional enforcement effort.[30] Fourth, in conjunction with the enforcement program, the amnesty would reconfigure the tax penalty schedule in a manner that would probably increase revenues both in the short run (because of the incentives to pay up) and in the long run (because paying old debts reduces future costs of compliance).

Our view of the world is summarized in Box 4. If these political prognostications are accepted, the relevant comparison when considering an amnesty will be between boxes A and D of Box 4, the status quo and a new regime offering an amnesty coupled with future strict enforcement.

Our review suggests that an effectively managed federal tax amnesty program combined with an advertised enhancement of enforcement might potentially raise significant revenue, perhaps about $10 billion, with continuing substantial revenue gains, albeit of highly uncertain magnitude. Although there are no guarantees such a program will work, the crude estimates of potential gains are large enough to warrant a full-fledged consideration of an amnesty program. And since each enforcement dollar yields many dollars in revenue, quite apart from its effects on nurturing compliance, if the discussion of amnesty merely pushes enforcement issues into Congressional debate, it will certainly have been worthwhile.

REFERENCES

Business Week, Coming clean: Tax amnesty may be heading for Washington. March 10, 1986, p. 31.

Jackson, Ira A. 1986. Amnesty and creative tax administration. *National Tax Journal* 39, no. 3: 317–24.

Lerman, Allen H. 1986. Tax amnesty: The federal perspective. *National Tax Journal* 39, no. 3:325–32.

Malanga, Frank. 1986. The relationship between IRS enforcement and tax yield. *National Tax Journal* 39, no. 3: 333–37.

Massachusetts Department of Revenue. 1986. Fair and firm federal tax administration. Mimeo. (May).

30. The IRS has not been run as a profit center and does not directly retain any of the revenue it collects. Tax reform proposals included a provision to permit the IRS to keep a fraction of its enforcement collections, but the specter of IRS agents overeager to collect from hapless taxpayers led to the rejection of this idea.

————. 1986. Massachusetts amnesty program: A statistical synopsis. Mimeo. (June).

Tax Foundation. 1986. Excises, amnesty, and fiscal foibles. Washington, D.C. Mimeo. (April).

U.S. Bureau of the Census. *State tax collections,* various years.

U.S. Department of Treasury, Internal Revenue Service. 1983. *Income tax compliance research: Estimates for 1973–1981.* Washington, D.C. (July).

Jeffrey E. Harris

Massachusetts Institute of Technology and Massachusetts General
Hospital

The 1983 Increase in the Federal
Cigarette Excise Tax

From 1951 through 1982, the U.S. federal excise tax on cigarettes remained at $0.08 per pack. As part of the Tax Equity and Fiscal Responsi-
bility Act of 1982, the U.S. Congress temporarily increased the tax to
$0.16 per pack, effective January 1, 1983. The statute contained a sunset
clause that provided for resumption of the old $0.08 rate on October 1,
1985. After a half-dozen temporary extensions, Congress made the $0.16
rate permanent in 1986.

In this paper, I take a closeup look at the microeconomics of the recent
federal cigarette tax increase. My main conclusions are as follows:

1. During 1981–1986, the real price of a pack of cigarettes, adjusted for
   general inflation, rose 36 percent.
2. Quantitatively, the main component of rising cigarette prices was *not*
   the increased federal excise tax, but a rapid expansion in the wholesale prices charged by the major U.S. cigarette manufacturers.
3. The pattern of manufacturers' wholesale price increases had many of
   the characteristics of an oligopoly price markup.
4. With the federal tax increase already scheduled, manufacturers' wholesale prices began to increase substantially in the fall of 1982, at least
   three months before the scheduled tax rise. From August 1982 through
   December 1983—as a result of six industry-wide price announcements—the wholesale prices of branded, nondiscount cigarettes rose

Research supported in part by Grant No. 1 RO3 CA-41117-01 from the U.S. National Cancer Institute, and by Grant No. PBR-18 from the American Cancer Society. The contents of
this paper are the author's sole responsibility.

$0.09 per pack, exclusive of the federal excise tax. There is little evidence that such price increases were matched by cost increases.

5. The preannounced, one-time federal tax increase appears to have served as a focal point for coordinating oligopoly price increases by sellers.

6. Accordingly, the full impact of the increase in the federal excise tax may not have been the legislated $0.08 per pack rise in price, but a market-induced jump in price of about $0.16 per pack. Quite contrary to the conventional view of the incidence of excise taxes, the federal excise tax may actually have had a multiplier effect upon price.

7. During 1981–1986, per capita consumption of cigarettes declined 15 percent. The increase in cigarette prices was probably the main cause of the decline.

8. The decline in cigarette use reflected mostly a decrease in the number of cigarette smokers rather than in the amount smoked by continuing users. The evidence supports the hypothesis that price increases do not induce smokers to cut down on the number of cigarettes. Instead, they either induce existing smokers to quit or prevent potential smokers from starting.

9. Even if a rise in the price of cigarettes reduces the number of smokers, there is insufficient evidence to determine whether the effect is reversible. We do not know whether quitters would resume smoking if the price were to fall, or whether more teenagers would start.

10. Who cuts down on cigarettes, who quits, and who fails to start are critical questions in assessing the quantitative effect of a cigarette tax increase on the health of the population. It is likely that, as a result of the price-induced decline in cigarette consumption during 1982–1985, about 100,000 additional persons will survive to age sixty-five.

The cigarette tax has already been studied, argued about, and reviewed. I hardly intend yet another review of the reviews. In particular, I do not inquire about the general role of excise taxes in federal tax policy, nor do I compare cigarette taxes to other federal excise taxes, such as those for the airport and highway trust funds. I do not ask whether increases in federal excise taxes usurp the states' taxing roles. For the year ending June 30, 1986, federal excise tax revenues on cigarettes were an estimated $4.4 billion,[1] constituting 13 percent of total federal excise tax

---

1. U.S. Department of Agriculture, Economic Research Service. *Tobacco situation and outlook report.* Number TS-195, September 1986, Table 31.

collections and 0.8 percent of total federal on-budget receipts.[2] Federal excise tax collections were about half of combined federal, state, and local governmental excise tax revenues from cigarettes.[3] For calendar 1985, total governmental excise tax collections on cigarettes comprised about 0.4 percent of personal consumption expenditures.[4] Although excise taxes make up less than 1 percent of governmental tax revenues in the United States, the proportion exceeds 5 percent in the United Kingdom and the Federal Republic of Germany (Gray and Walter (1986)).

Moreover, I shall not consider the direct incidence of cigarette excise taxation. Although one repeatedly hears that cigarette taxes are income regressive, it needs to be understood that regressivity is only one dimension of fairness. In a 1980–1981 survey, expenditures on tobacco by consumers in the lowest income quintile constituted 1.2 percent of their total expenditures and 2.9 percent of their income; for the highest income quartile, tobacco made up 0.7 percent of total expenditures and 0.5 percent of income.[5] From a 1978–1980 series, I have computed cigarette excise tax payments to be 0.5 percent of income for adults under age sixty-five, but only 0.3 percent of income for the elderly (Harris (1986)). Although an estimated 31 percent of adults are current smokers,[6] one survey of business executives found that only 14 percent of top managers now smoke cigarettes.[7,8]

1. Price and Consumption in the Modern Cigarette Industry

Figure 1 depicts the relation between consumption and price of cigarettes during the twenty-three year period since the 1964 issuance of the report of the Surgeon General's Advisory Committee on smoking and health. The quantity of cigarettes is the annual consumption per person aged eighteen and over. (It is not consumption per adult smoker, but

---

2. U.S. Department of Treasury. *U.S. Treasury Bulletin.* 3rd quarter, fiscal 1986. Table FFO-2.
3. U.S. Department of Agriculture, Economic Research Service. *Tobacco situation and outlook report.* Number TS-195, September 1986, Table 31.
4. *Economic report of the president.* February 1986, Table B-14.
5. U.S. Department of Labor, Bureau of Labor Statistics. Consumer expenditure survey: Results from the 1980–81 interview. *News Release,* December 19, 1984, Table 1, reproduced in Toder (1986).
6. U.S. National Center for Health Statistics. Provisional data from the National Health Interview Survey: United States, January–June 1985. *Advance data from vital and health statistics.* Number 119, May 14, 1986.
7. Robert Half International, Inc., New York, 1986.
8. See also Chappell (1985), Shughart and Savarese (1986), Toder (1986), Harris (1982, 1986).

consumption per adult.) The price is given in dollars per pack, converted by the Consumer Price Index to constant 1986 prices.[9]

The price-quantity relation in Figure 1 slopes neither uniformly downward like a demand curve nor uniformly upward like a supply curve. What Figure 1 shows is the combined effects of movements in both the supply curve and the demand curve for cigarettes. In general, one can-

---

9. The horizontal axis in Figure 1 represents total U.S. consumption per person aged eighteen and over, as reported by the U.S. Department of Agriculture. The vertical axis represents the real mean domestic price per pack in constant 1986 dollars. To obtain current mean prices, I divided consumer expenditures for cigarettes (compiled from reports of the U.S. Department of Commerce, Bureau of Economic Analysis) by total U.S. consumption exclusive of overseas forces (as estimated by the U.S. Department of Agriculture, Economic Research Service). The 1986 data are provisional. See U.S. Department of Agriculture. *Tobacco situation and outlook reports,* various issues.

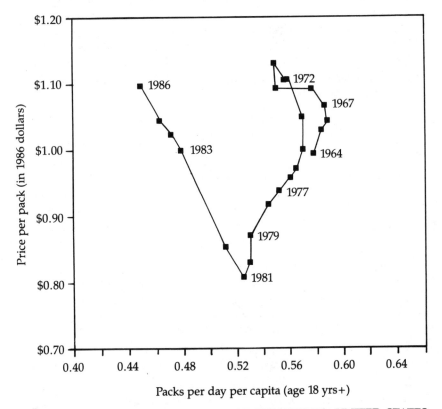

Figure 1 PRICE AND CONSUMPTION OF CIGARETTES, UNITED STATES, 1964–1966

not sort out these separate supply and demand effects merely from the type of data given in the figure. However, with additional information about market conditions, one could reconstruct a meaningful story of the separate influences of supply and demand in the modern American cigarette market.

It is useful to divide Figure 1 into three historical phases according to the movement of real prices: an initial period of price increases (1964–1971); a subsequent period of price declines (1971–1981); and a most recent period of renewed price increases (1981–1986).

1964–1971 The first phase was dominated by two main influences: actions by public and private organizations to publicize the health hazards of cigarette smoking; and increases in state and local cigarette excise taxes.

Thus, following the 1964 Surgeon General's report, the first required health warning on cigarette advertising and packages became law in July 1966.[10] In November 1967, the Federal Trade Commission issued its first periodic report on "tar" and nicotine contents of various brands. In March 1969, the Federal Communications Commission, applying the Fairness Doctrine, ruled that television stations must present a significant number of antismoking messages during prime-time viewing hours when cigarette commercials were presented. In April 1970,[11] Congress strengthened the required health warning and banned the broadcast of cigarette advertising starting January 2, 1971. (See Harris (1979)).

Concomitantly, during 1964–1971, the nominal price of cigarettes increased by about $0.13 per pack, about half of which represented increases in state and local excise taxes. Had there been no changes in state and local taxes during that period, the real price of cigarettes would have changed very little.

Much econometric sweat has poured forth in assigning the relative influence of health information and state taxes in the 1964–1971 phase, particularly in the drop in consumption during 1967–1970.[12] All of these efforts point to the same conclusion: increases in excise taxes pushed the supply curve upward, and emerging health information pushed the demand curve back.

1971–1981 The second phase has been somewhat more resistant to simple interpretation. Cigarette demand, according to some observers,

10. Federal Cigarette Labelling and Advertising Act (Public Law 89–92).
11. Public Health Cigarette Smoking Act (Public Law 91–222).
12. See, for example, Hamilton (1974), Schneider, Klein, and Murphy (1981), Porter (1985), Bishop and Yoo (1985), and Baltagi and Levin (1986).

rebounded after the 1971 ban on cigarette advertising and the concomitant removal of antismoking messages from the prime-time viewing hours (e.g., Hamilton (1974)). Others note that cigarette advertising expenditures, though declining in real terms for a few years after the ban, rebounded as the manufacturers intensified their promotional events and expenditures on nonelectronic media (U.S. Federal Trade Commission (1984)). On the supply side, the growth of state and local excise taxes slowed considerably: the absolute increase in nominal excise taxes per pack during 1971–1981 was less than half of the rise for 1964–1971.

Moreover, the average cigarette was being produced at progressively lower cost. These declines in unit cost appear to have resulted mainly from product changes as opposed to pure improvements in technical efficiency. Thus, from 1971 to 1981, the domestic market share of "low tar" cigarettes increased from 4 to 56 percent (U.S. Federal Trade Commission (1984)). Concomitantly, the average quantity of tobacco per cigarette fell by 16 percent.[13]

Accordingly, diminishing real excise taxes and absolutely declining production costs pushed the supply curve for cigarettes back downward during the 1970s. The demand curve probably continued to shift back as well. The net effect was a marked decline in price with relatively unchanged consumption.

1981–1986 During the third and most recent period, the real price of cigarettes rebounded almost to its peak of 1970. The biggest jump was from 1982 to 1983, the latter being the year of the federal tax increase.

Table 1 shows the separate components of the retail price of cigarettes from 1978 through 1985. The total price is broken down into four parts: the federal cigarette excise tax; the average state and local excise tax; the wholesale price quoted by cigarette manufacturers (exclusive of excise taxes); and the remaining retail trade markup. In contrast to Figure 1, the table shows the nominal prices in each year, uncorrected for general price inflation.

To interpret the evidence in Table 1, we need some institutional details. Cigarette manufacturers sell their products to regional distributors. Upon transit from the manufacturers to the distributors' warehouses, the federal excise tax is paid. (Some cigarette shipments, such as to the military and Indian reservations, are federal tax exempt. There are also inventory or "floor stock" taxes, to which I shall return). By convention,

13. Calculated from U.S. Department of Agriculture, Economic Research Service, *Tobacco situation and outlook report*, Number TS-175, March 1981, Table 2 and Number TS-196, September 1986. I computed the average weight of tobacco per cigarette to be 998 mg in 1964, 840 mg in 1971, 707 mg in 1981, and 621 mg per cigarette in 1986.

the manufacturers' prices are quoted inclusive of the federal tax. Such prices, typically per 1,000 cigarettes, may differ by brand category (non-filter, king size, 100 mm, etc.). When the cigarettes enter specific states for retail sale, the state tax, as applicable, is to be paid. Regional distributors, wholesalers, and retailers (vending machine operators, supermarkets, etc.) attach further markups, some of which are governed by fair trade laws in the respective states. What Table 1 shows is each of these effects as well as their total.

Superficially, Table 1 shows that the main source of the 1982–1983 price rise was the increase in the federal excise tax. However, for the entire period 1981–1985, the main source of increased prices is the manufacturers' wholesale price of cigarettes, and not rising excise taxes. For example, during 1981–1985, the average retail price of cigarettes rose from $0.67 to $1.03 per pack. Of this nominal price rise of $0.36 per pack, $0.08 was due to the federal excise tax; $0.03 to rising state and local taxes; $0.08 to retail trade markups; and the remaining $0.17 to manufacturers.[14]

Put differently, the 1981–1985 period represented a 30 percent increase in the real price of a pack of cigarettes. If the federal excise tax had not been increased during 1981–1985, but all other components of price remained as in Table 1, then the real price of cigarettes would still have increased 20 percent.

Figure 2 reinterprets the data in Table 1. In contrast to the table, the time periods are fiscal years ending June 30. During fiscal year 1983, the

14. As a check on the accuracy of the estimated manufacturers' wholesale prices, I performed the following alternative computations for a single domestic cigarette manufacturer—Lorillard, Inc.

Year	Cigarette revenues ($ billion)	Federal excise taxes paid ($ billion)	Estimated wholesale price per pack ($)
1978	0.813	0.218	0.22
1979	0.951	0.235	0.24
1980	1.053	0.239	0.27
1981	1.109	0.228	0.31
1982	1.173	0.213	0.36
1983	1.490	0.429	0.40
1984	1.431	0.383	0.44
1985	1.501	0.378	0.48

Total cigarette revenues and total federal excise taxes paid were derived from the annual reports of Loews Corporation, of which Lorillard is a subsidiary. The estimated wholesale price per pack is computed from the formula $t(R - T)/T$, where R is total cigarette revenues, T is total federal excise tax payments, and t is the federal excise tax rate per pack ($0.08 in 1978–1982, $0.16 in 1983–1985).

Table 1 CHANGES IN CIGARETTE PRICES, BY COMPONENT
UNITED STATES, 1978–1985

	Mean retail price	Federal excise tax	State & local tax	Manufact. wholesale price	Other retail markups
1978	0.55	0.08	0.12	0.22	0.12
1979	0.58	0.08	0.13	0.24	0.13
1980	0.63	0.08	0.13	0.27	0.14
1981	0.67	0.08	0.13	0.31	0.15
1982	0.75	0.08	0.13	0.37	0.17
1983	0.91	0.16	0.15	0.40	0.19
1984	0.97	0.16	0.15	0.44	0.22
1985	1.03	0.16	0.16	0.48	0.23

All prices and components in current dollars per pack. State and local tax equals state and local tax
revenues divided by domestic consumption. The manufacturers' wholesale price equals the weighted
average of wholesale prices (exclusive of federal excise tax), where the weights reflect the proportion of
the year that each quoted price was in effect; the proportion of output for each brand (standard, king
size 85mm, filter 80mm, 100mm, and 120mm); and the market share of the manufacturer. Computation
of the mean wholesale prices includes generic and discount brands, whose market shares were 0.9 percent in 1982, 3.3 percent in 1983, 5.5 percent in 1984, and 7.3 percent in 1985. Other retail markups are
computed as residuals.

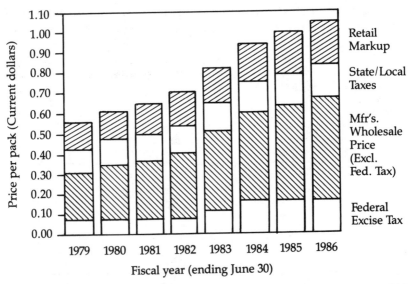

Figure 2 CIGARETTE PRICES BY COMPONENT, FISCAL YEARS 1979–1986

manufacturers' wholesale price increased by $0.07 per pack. By contrast, the federal excise tax (in effect only for half of the fiscal year) increased by about $0.04 per pack. During fiscal 1982 through fiscal 1984, increases in manufacturers' wholesale prices constituted about half of the retail price increase.

THE 1982 PRICE INCREASE

The key datum, it appears, is the behavior of manufacturers' wholesale price in the second half of calendar 1982, before the federal tax increase was to take effect.

Table 2 sets forth such information in detail. The table gives the behavior of manufacturers' wholesale prices for their higher-priced 100 mm brands, inclusive of federal excise taxes, from September 29, 1982, through June 27, 1985. The table indicates the dates of announcement of price increases; which firms announced the price increases on the first day of the announcement period (the "leading firms(s)"); which firms followed suit with price increases ("responding firms(s)"); and the list prices, net of the announced price increases, for each of the six major firms that comprise the domestic cigarette market. (The price increases announced during December 10–17, 1982, were effective January 3, 1983. Otherwise, all announcements were effective immediately or within a few days.)

Prior to 1982, manufacturers had typically announced coincident wholesale price increases twice annually. From 1975 to 1982, such prices were essentially uniform across manufacturers. The situation changed in 1982. In February 1982 (not shown in Table 2), all manufacturers' list prices increased uniformly by $1.00 to $21.70 per 1,000. Again, during August–September 1982 (also not shown in Table 2), manufacturers increased their list prices, but for the first time by differing amounts: Philip Morris by $1.40 to $23.10; the other five firms by $2.00 to $23.70.[15]

All firms again increased prices during September 29 through October 2, 1982, again by differing amounts. Concurrently, manufacturers announced "tax assistance plans" to ease the transition through the scheduled January 1 tax increase.[16] Such plans offered limited, tempo-

15. As of this writing, I have not located the individual manufacturers' telegrams announcing the February 1982 and August–September 1982 wholesale price increases; hence, they do not appear in Table 2. Data on median increases in wholesale price are given in U.S. Department of Agriculture. *Tobacco situation and outlook report*. Number TS-196, September 1986, Table 5. See also Number TS-177, September 1981.

16. R. J. Reynolds announced its Federal Excise Tax Assistance Plan (FETAP) on October 2, 1982: "In view of the impending federal excise tax increase on cigarettes, we have developed a program to help offset the impact of the increase for direct accounts and retailers and reduce the impact of higher prices on consumers. RJR's programs will

Table 2 PATTERN OF MANUFACTURERS' WHOLESALE PRICE INCREASES FOR 100MM BRANDS SEPTEMBER 29, 1982 THROUGH JUNE 27, 1985

| Announcement period | | Leading Firm(s) | Responding Firm(s) | Post-increase price ($ per 1000) | | | | | |
From	To			AM	BW	LM	LO	PM	RJ
29 Sep 82	06 Oct 82	LO	All	25.70	25.20	25.70	25.20	25.20	25.70
11 Nov 82	16 Nov 82	BW	Not RJ	27.20	26.20	27.20	27.20	27.20	25.70
10 Dec 82	17 Dec 82	PM, RJ	All	27.90	27.90	27.90	27.90	28.90	27.90
17 Jun 83	22 Jun 83	RJ	All	29.40	29.40	29.40	29.40	29.40	29.40
16 Dec 83	19 Dec 83	5 firms	All	30.15	30.15	30.15	30.15	30.15	30.15
01 Jun 84	06 Jun 84	PM	All	31.15	31.15	31.15	31.15	31.15	31.15
14 Dec 84	17 Dec 84	PM, RJ	All	32.40	32.40	32.40	32.40	32.15	32.40
29 Jan 85	29 Jan 85	PM	None	32.40	32.40	32.40	32.40	32.40	32.40
13 Jun 85	14 Jun 85	PM, RJ	All	33.40	33.40	33.40	33.40	33.05	33.40
27 Jun 85	27 Jun 85	PM	None	33.40	33.40	33.40	33.40	33.40	33.40

Source: Telegrams by manufacturers to wholesalers.
Note: Prices include applicable federal excise tax. Federal excise tax increased from $4.00 to $8.00 per 1000 cigarettes effective January 1, 1983. AM = American Tobacco Co.; BW = Brown & Williamson Tobacco Corp.; LM = Liggett & Myers Tobacco Co.; LO = Lorillard Inc.; PM = Philip Morris USA; RJ = R. J. Reynolds Tobacco Co.

rary bonus payments for accelerated purchases, as well as discounts to offset federal taxes on year-end inventories.[17] Moreover, several firms began to introduce generic and discounted brands.[18] Still, the net effect was to raise prices in 1982, not 1983. By the end of 1982, through five successive increases in list prices ($0.02 per pack in February, $0.04 per pack in August, $0.04 per pack in October, $0.03 per pack in November, and $0.014 per pack in December), the $0.08 per-pack tax increase had been almost twice recovered.

By June 1983, interfirm divergences in wholesale price had been virtually eliminated. In December 1984 and June 1985, Philip Morris's initial price increase fell short of that announced by R. J. Reynolds, which the remaining four firms followed. In both instances, Philip Morris acted within two weeks to match the others' price.

However, as the excise tax approached sunset on October 1, 1985, a new phase was entered. On September 13, 1985, Philip Morris announced a program to rebate taxes due on floor stocks should the federal tax expire as scheduled and should no provision be made for a floor stock tax refund. On September 19, American Tobacco Company offered to rebate the differential on one week's average supply should the tax expire and "the federal government does not provide for a floor stock tax refund to manufacturers and wholesalers. . . ." On September 18 and 20, R. J. Reynolds offered a similar one-week refund (its Federal Excise Tax Reduction Protection Plan) if "the federal government does not provide a tax refund to wholesalers or manufacturers. . . ." On September 19, 1985, Lorillard announced an "inventory protection" plan to take effect if the federal excise tax should expire as scheduled and if "the Bu-

---

generate funds for direct accounts to assist in offsetting the year end floor tax and higher 1983 capital requirements. Retailers and consumers will benefit from unprecedented promotion programs throughout the remainder of 1982." Thereafter, the circular explained that a $2.00 increase would go into effect immediately, representing one half of the anticipated $4.00 increase. R. J. Reynolds's next price increase, announced December 10, 1982, was for $2.20, which, it explained, constituted $2.00 as the second half of the $4.00 tax increase and $0.20 for "the costs associated with increased working capital and the 3¼% discount related to the higher federal excise tax." The October 1, 1982 increase of $2.00, R. J. Reynolds stated, was "an effort to minimize the impact to customers of doubling the federal excise tax by recovering the higher tax in two steps."

17. Philip Morris USA appears to have instituted a "Floor Tax Protection Plan" in October, 1982. Brown & Williamson established an "Excise Tax Protection Plan," along with assumption of the floor tax, in December 1982.

18. On October 6, 1982, Liggett & Myers announced a price increase on all regular brands, but exclusive of private label and generic brands marketed by Gary Tobacco Company, a subsidiary of Liggett. In a mailing two days later, Liggett asked wholesalers to advertise Gary brands aggressively.

reau of Alcohol, Tobacco and Firearms does not allow a rebate of the [federal excise tax] reduction on manufacturers' and wholesalers' inventory on hand. . . ." Subsequently, the Congress extended the excise tax temporarily to November 15, 1985. And likewise, between October 31 and November 9, firms announced similar tax protection plans.

These nearly simultaneous announcements may be more salient for what they did not say. None of the announcements mentioned the possibility of a permanent price decrease should the federal tax sunset. They may have been intended to indicate that no such decrease was contemplated.

COSTS AND PROFITS

Why did wholesale prices increase? There is little if any evidence of comparably increased costs. During the 1980s, the average quantity of tobacco per cigarette continued to decline. Moreover, imported tobacco became an increasingly significant portion of all tobacco used in American cigarettes. Such imported tobacco, mostly Oriental leaf, cost considerably less than domestic tobacco even with ocean freight and import duties, in part because of domestic price supports and in part because the entire Oriental leaf is usable without stemming.

To be sure, advertising and promotional expenditures of tobacco manufacturers rose from $1.55 billion to $2.10 billion during 1981–1984 (U.S. Federal Trade Commission (1986)). However, this cost increase, equaling $0.55 billion in aggregate, amounted to only $0.022 per pack. During the same period, manufacturers' wholesale price (exclusive of the excise tax) rose by about $0.13 per pack (Table 1).

American cigarette manufacturers are conglomerate, multinational firms. Accordingly, data on aggregate profits by company, or even profits by tobacco line of business (combined domestic and international) may not be indicative of profits solely from domestic cigarette sales. Moreover, reports of accounting profits for particular lines of business can be affected by methods of allocating corporatewide expenses. Still, the data that are available do not support the view that manufacturers' wholesale price increases reflected a comparable rise in the costs of operation.

Thus, for 1981 to 1985, the combined operating profits of Philip Morris, R. J. Reynolds, American Brands, and Loews Corporation from their tobacco lines of business (domestic and international) rose from $2.98 billion to $4.77 billion (annual reports of respective companies). These four companies held a combined domestic market share in excess of 80 percent during this period.

Similarly, from 1980 to 1985, Philip Morris USA, the domestic tobacco subsidiary of Philip Morris Companies, Inc. and the largest domestic manufacturer, achieved the following unit sales and operating income:[19]

	Unit Sales (billions of packs)	Operating income ($ billion)	Operating income per pack ($)
1980	9.56	0.79	.082
1981	9.97	0.91	.091
1982	10.22	1.10	.108
1983	10.23	1.34	.131
1984	10.58	1.75	.165
1985	10.68	2.05	.192

Thus, for Philip Morris USA during 1980–1985, operating income increased by $0.11 per pack. During the same period, manufacturers' wholesale prices (including discounts and generic cigarettes, but excluding excise taxes) rose by an estimated $0.21 per pack (Table 1). These data suggest that about one half of the manufacturers' price increase during 1980–1985 can be accounted for by increased unit costs.

The evidence thus indicates that during 1981–1985, American cigarette manufacturers raised wholesale prices—exclusive of excise tax payments—by $0.17 per pack. Such a price increase was coincident with a one-time increase of $0.08 per pack in the federal excise tax, announced in 1982 and effective beginning in 1983. A key question is whether the preannounced federal tax increase served, at least in part, as a means to effectuate the rise in wholesale price.

EXCISE TAXES AND OLIGOPOLY BEHAVIOR

The cigarette industry has been repeatedly cited as an example of an imperfectly competitive industry. In the famous Tobacco Case of 1946, the major cigarette manufacturers were convicted of operating an illegal cartel in the 1930s (Nicholls (1949)). Although manufacturers were convicted, the consensus has been that company behavior was not changed by the verdict. Today, the American cigarette market remains a six-firm oligopoly. In 1982, the top four firms held a combined market share of 87 percent; the Herfindahl Index was 2543 (Porter (1986)).

How would the imposition of an excise tax affect the retail price of a

19. See Philip Morris Companies, Inc. *1985 Annual report*. See also Moody's Investor's Service, *Moody's industrial manual*, 1982, p. 3246; 1983, p. 3261; 1984, p. 3272; 1986, p. 3351. Operating income equals operating revenues net of excise taxes, cost of sales, and depreciation. It does not include deductions for income taxes, interest expense, corporate expense, and other nonoperating income and deductions.

product sold in an oligopoly market? In general, there are two basic approaches to answering this question.

The first approach is to specify the rules of interaction among the sellers and then to analyze the effect of the tax *given* such rules. Thus, we determine the effect of a tax increase if the oligopoly operated as a cartel; alternatively, we assess the effect of the same tax increase if the firms showed no collusive or interdependent behavior; and finally, we assess the same effect if the member firms displayed partial interdependence. Each set of rules would give a different result. For example, for a competitive industry with perfectly elastic supply, all of the tax would be passed on to consumers. The logical inverse of this approach is that if we have already observed the response of an industry to an excise tax increase, then we could work backward to infer the degree of interdependence among the sellers. With such an approach in mind, some economists have studied how retail cigarette prices vary in relation to excise taxes across states (Sumner (1981), Bulow and Pfleiderer (1983), Sullivan (1985), Barzel (1976)).

The second approach does not take the rules of firm interaction as given. Instead, the idea is that the imposition of the excise tax may actually change the rules. That is, the tax increase could allow firms to act more like a cartel; alternatively, it could be the event that disrupts a collusive arrangement.

Within this second approach, there are two lines of reasoning. The first focuses on the incentives of would-be cartel members to cheat. The idea is that the imposition of an excise tax threatens profit margins in the same way as an increase in production costs. In turn, the profit situation in the industry affects the stability of any collusive or partially collusive arrangement. Although economists have long held that shrinking profit margins threaten such collusive arrangements, there is now some evidence to the contrary (Rotemberg and Saloner (1986)). Smaller profits, it appears, reduce the reward to recalcitrant behavior, and thus firms stick together.

Alternatively, the tax increase serves as a "focal point" or "coordinating device." The idea is that in a world where explicit, written contracts to fix prices are illegal, sellers will seek other bases for implicit agreement. The classic example is the phases of the moon, used by one cartel to determine whose turn it was to win in a series of supposedly sealed-bid auctions. Member firms used such an external event to coordinate behavior without explicitly communicating with each other.

A pending excise tax increase, which is scheduled to go into effect in a national market at a fixed rate on a fixed date, could in principle serve as such a coordinating device. Firms would announce a price increase in anticipation of the pending tax hike. Because the pending tax increase is fixed and predictable, such firms would have good reason to anticipate that other industry members will respond likewise. An ideal but subtle strategy would be to implement the price increases in successive increments, each time assessing whether other firms will match the price rise. So long as prices were not already at fully collusive levels, member firms could push prices well beyond the magnitude of the tax increase.

The tax increase would act as a cover for the price increases. That is, during the period surrounding the tax increases, consumers may have difficulty discerning what proportion of the ultimate retail price increase was due to the tax. Such an effect would be enhanced if the industry operated through complex lines of distribution, involving multiple wholesalers and retailers, all of whom append their own markups to the ultimate price.

The behavior of the American cigarette industry during the period surrounding the federal excise tax increase is consistent with the hypothesis that the tax increase served as a focal point for an oligopolistic price increase. Prices increased in late 1982, the period prior to the effective date of the tax. Sellers justified such premature increases as smoothing the transition for wholesalers and ultimate consumers. The price increases occurred by a sequence of increments (August 1982, September 1982, October 1982, December 1982, etc.), in which an announcement by one firm would trigger responses by others. Although there were pr ce differences for a few months before and after January 1, 1983, the date that the tax went into effect, such price differences were virtually eliminated by June 1983. Most of the price increases were initiated by Philip Morris and R. J. Reynolds, the two largest firms in the industry. During December 1984 and June 1985, when an initial increase announced by Philip Morris was more than matched by other firms, Philip Morris soon brought its price in line. During the period when the excise tax was pending expiration, firms made a sequence of announcements that failed to suggest any possibility that after-tax prices to wholesalers might fall. The pending sunset of the tax appears to have served as a focal point to communicate to other firms that prices would not be cut.

MULTIPLIER EFFECTS OF THE FEDERAL EXCISE TAX INCREASE

There is now an ambiguity about the impact of the federal excise tax on prices, which will necessarily carry over to its impact on consumption and, in fact, on health. The evidence indicates that an oligopoly price increase occurred. If the oligopoly price increase would have occurred in the absence of a federal tax hike, then the increase in the federal excise tax may conceivably have had a negligible effect on price. That is, manufacturers would have raised wholesale prices to the point where retail prices are exactly as they are now. Alternatively, if the tax was a critical focal point for coordinating an oligopoly price increase, than the increase in the federal tax had a multiplier effect on price.

The value of this multiplier effect could not be computed precisely from the data on hand. We would need to know how much sellers would have increased price without the tax. We would also have to determine what would have happened to retail markups. From the available evidence, the multiplier effect could be as large as twofold. That is, an $0.08 increase in the federal excise tax actually led to about $0.16 increase in retail price.

2. Taxes and Cigarette Consumption

During 1981–1986, as shown in Figure 1, the real price of cigarettes increased by 36 percent. Concomitantly, per capita consumption declined by 15 percent.

Was the decline in consumption simply a response to the rise in price, or were there other superimposed trends in demand? Put differently, does the downward-sloping portion of the price-quantity diagram in Figure 1 (that is, from 1986 to 1981) represent a piece of the current market demand curve?

One crude test is to compute the demand price elasticity from the putative segment of a demand curve in Figure 1 and compare it to other estimates in the literature. From Figure 1, we obtain that every 1 percent increase in the real price results in about a 42 percent decline in consumption (that is, $^{15}/_{36}$). Although estimates of price elasticity have varied from 20 to 120 percent, the above value of 42 percent falls pretty much in the consensus range of 40–70 percent (Toder (1986)).

The difficulty with simple computations based upon the price elasticity is that other economic variables have changed since 1981. During 1981–1984, for example, per capita consumption declined 10 percent while the real price of cigarettes increased by 27 percent. Concomitantly, cigarette manufacturers' advertising and promotional expenditures rose in real terms by 18 percent, and real disposable personal income rose by 10 percent. A more sophisticated test of the effect of price increases on demand would take account of these additional factors.

Such a test is performed in Table 3. The first row shows the actual percentage decline in per capita consumption during 1981–1984 (that is, from 0.525 to 0.472 packs per day per capita). The remaining rows in the table show what each of six different econometric analyses of the demand curve for cigarettes would have predicted for 1984. For each model, two predictions are given: the percentage decline during 1981–1984 if only price had changed; and the corresponding percentage decline in consumption, taking into account such additional factors as income and advertising.[20]

With the exception of the Lewit–Coate model, the predicted overall declines in cigarette consumption were less than the "price effect only"

20. Let C denote per capita consumption of cigarettes; P, the real price per pack; Y, real per capita disposable income; A, real advertising and promotional expenditures of cigarette manufacturers; S, the stock of "advertising capital," a time series in which past contributions to the stock depreciate at a rate of one third per year; L, the fraction of cigarettes consumed with FTC tar rating below 15 mg; T, average tobacco per cigarette; C_{-1}, one-year lagged consumption per capita; POP, the total adult population eighteen and over; and YR, the calendar year.

The prediction equations were as follows. For Schneider et al. (1981, equation (8)): $\log (C) = \text{constant} - 1.218 \log (P) + 0.462 \log (Y) + 0.046 \log(S) - 0.235L - 1.386 \log(T)$. For Porter (1986, Table 6, equation (4)): $\log(C) = \text{constant} - 0.290 \log(P) - 0.130 \log(Y) + 0.0909 \log(S) - 0.390L - 0.319 \log(T)$. For Baltagi and Levin (1986, Table 1, OLS): $\log C = \text{constant} - 0.225 \log(P) + 0.004 \log (Y) + 0.038 \log(A) + 0.927 \log (C_{-1})$. For Ippolito et al. (1979, Table 1, equation (1)): $\log(C) = \text{constant} - 0.811 \log(P) + 0.735 \log(Y) - 0.014\text{YR}$. For Bishop and Yoo (1985, Table I, 3SLS): $\log(C \cdot \text{POP}) = \text{constant} - 0.454 \cdot \log(P) + 0.919 \cdot \log(Y) + 0.095 \cdot \log(A)$. For Lewit and Coate (1982, Table 2 Restricted Sample): $C = 0.779 - 0.315P$.

Except for the linear model of Lewit–Coate, the econometric analyses predicted the logarithm of consumption. Accordingly, it is more appropriate to assess the proportional change in consumption during 1981–1984, as is done in Table 3. For the Lewit–Coate model, I adjusted the "constant" term in the model so that, at a real price of $0.807 in 1981, the observed consumption of 0.525 packs/day per capita would be predicted.

Table 3 ACTUAL VERSUS PREDICTED DECLINE IN PER CAPITA
CONSUMPTION, 1981–1984: SIX ECONOMETRIC MODELS

	Percent decline in per capita consumption, 1981–1984	
	Price effect only	Overall effect
Actual decline		10
Predicted decline		
Bishop and Yoo (1985)	10	5
Porter (1986)	7	5
Baltagi and Levin (1986)	11	10
Lewit and Coate (1982)	13	13
Ippolito et al. (1979)	18	16
Schneider et al. (1981)	25	21

The methods of calculation are given in footnote 20.

estimates. That is, such factors as rising incomes and advertising were expected to counteract the demand-depressing effect of price increases. For the three models that included more recent data (Bishop and Yoo (1985), Porter (1986), Baltagi and Levin (1986)), I find that the "price only" predictions show a consumption decline ranging from 7 to 11 percent, whereas the overall predictions show a decline ranging from 5 to 10 percent.

I thus conclude that most of the decline during 1981–1984 could be explained on the basis of price increases alone. However, unmeasured trends in cigarette consumption could also be important. From the Bishop–Yoo results, I decompose the observed 10 percent decline in consumption into three counteracting effects: a 10 percent decline due to price increases; an additional 5 percent decline due to secular trends in consumption; and an offsetting 5 percent increase due to rising incomes and increased cigarette advertising and promotion.

The unit for measuring demand in Figure 1 is consumption per capita, not consumption per smoker. Accordingly, changes in per capita consumption could reflect changes in either the average number smoked by current smokers or the proportion of smokers in the adult population.

Recent econometric studies of cigarette smoking in relation to local price levels (Lewit, Coate, and Grossman (1981), Lewit and Coate (1982)) have suggested that increases in price actually affect the proportion of smokers more than they affect the number smoked by continuing smokers. For adults, the demand price elasticity for the proportion of smokers was estimated to be 26 percent out of a total price elasticity of

Table 4   CIGARETTE USE IN RELATION TO PRICE FOR SELECTED YEARS, UNITED STATES, 1965–1985

Year	Price per pack ($1986)	Proportion of adults smoking cigarettes (%)	Average number of cigarettes per day per adult smoker
1965	1.03	42	28
1967	1.06	40	29
1970	1.14	37	30
1976	0.96	37	31
1978	0.92	33	33
1980	0.83	34	31
1983	1.00	32	30
1985	1.05	31	30

Sources: U.S. Department of Health and Human Services (1984); U.S. National Center for Health Statistics (1985, 1986); Harris (1980b).

42 percent. This estimated effect was found to be particularly striking among teenagers: the demand price elasticity for the proportion of smokers was 120 percent out of a total price elasticity of 140 percent.

Table 4 examines the national data on the proportion of smokers. For selected years, I have juxtaposed the price data of Figure 1 against survey-derived estimates of the proportion of adults who currently smoke cigarettes. I derived the rightmost column—the average daily consumption among adult current users—by dividing cigarette consumption per capita (as in Figure 1) by the proportion of current cigarette smokers given in the table. (Numerical adjustments to take teenage smoking into account lead to only minor changes in the rightmost column that do not alter the main conclusions.)

The patterns displayed in Table 4 show a reasonable but imperfect parallel to the aggregate per capita data in Figure 1. The prevalence of cigarette smoking fell during the late 1960s. (The decline was mostly from quitting smoking, though there may have been a reduction in the rate at which teenagers started to smoke. See Harris (1979, 1980b, 1983).) During the 1970s, the proportion of smokers declined less consistently. Moreover, as the market share of "low tar" cigarettes increased, the average daily smoking frequency showed a compensatory increase. During the 1980s, the prevalence of smoking declined in about the same proportion as per capita consumption. Accordingly, if the decline in consumption observed during the 1980s was caused mostly by price increases, then it was indeed an effect of price on the percentage of smokers.

How could price increases affect individual smoking in an all-or-none way? It is likely to be an interaction between prices and other influences on cigarette use. Surveys indicate that substantial proportions of cigarette smokers report recurrent unsuccessful attempts to quit smoking—sometimes five or more annually—in the face of an acknowledged desire to stop. Such attempts, which are typically very short-lived, are triggered no doubt by a variety of stimuli. Perhaps price increases trigger new attempts or improve the success rate of such attempts.

Given the data on cigarette prices, the price elasticity of demand for cigarettes, and the prevalence of smoking, one could estimate an independent quantitative effect of an $0.08-per-pack price increase (Harris (1982), Warner (1986)). As already noted, however, there is a conceptual question as to whether $0.08 is the correct quantity. If the change in the federal excise tax actually induced a full $0.16-per-pack increase in the nominal price of cigarettes, then I compute that, as a result of the federal excise tax increase and the resultant oligopoly response, about 2 million adults stopped smoking and 600,000 teenagers (aged 12–17) did not start.

3. Health Consequences

What will be the health consequences of the price-induced decline in smoking? Any attempt at a full response would require a separate paper. Instead, I shall offer the following points.

Cigarette smoke is a complex mixture of chemicals consumed at diverse stages of life. A reduction in smoking will have different effects on a woman of childbearing age, a young man trying to improve his exercise tolerance, a women in her thirties who takes oral contraceptives, a man who has worked for years with asbestos, or a man who already has poor circulation in his legs. These effects are qualitatively and quantitatively very different.

Moreover, responsiveness to price may vary considerably across smokers. To assess the health consequences of price increases, one therefore needs to know not merely the average price responsiveness of the smoking population, but whether price sensitivity is correlated with health effects (Harris (1980a)). We thus need to determine whether a newly pregnant smoking woman is more or less responsive to price increases than a smoker who, say, already has irreversible, terminal cancer.

At least for a number of chronic illnesses, the reversibility of smoking-induced danger depends on the duration of prior cigarette use. We thus need to know whether older persons who have smoked for several decades are more or less price sensitive than younger smokers. Further, there is evidence that for lung cancer the carcinogenic effect of the second pack of cigarettes per day may exceed that of the first pack (Doll and Peto (1978)). In that case, a heavy smoker's cutting down on a consumption might avert more damage than a moderate smoker's quitting. On the other hand, there may be illnesses for which the first cigarette of the day is more damaging than the last one.

Even if cigarette use responds relatively quickly to price increases, some of the health consequences of the resulting changes in smoking could take decades to be manifest. Thus, one's excess risk of lung cancer may not return to that of the nonsmoker for more than a decade. Abnormalities in the small airways of the lung, detectable in many of the youngest initiates to smoking, may indeed be rapidly reversible. But once chronic lung obstruction sets in, reversal of breathing impairment is much slower. By contrast, the effects of quitting smoking during pregnancy may be more immediate.

Moreover, predicting the future health consequences of current changes in smoking is hardly as easy as measuring the current health consequences of past changes in smoking. The median age of a person now dying from a disease caused by his cigarette smoking is about seventy years. Such an individual, roughly speaking, started to smoke in the early 1930s, may have switched to filtertip cigarettes in the 1950s and 1960s, and may have quit smoking in the past couple of years. Epidemiological and biomedical investigations have yielded substantial quantitative information about the health risks of cigarettes among such past users. In particular, such investigations have indicated that smokers of exclusively filtertip cigarettes of the type available during the 1960s incurred lower risks of lung cancer (and possibly other cancers) than smokers of nonfilter cigarettes. By contrast, the evidence that the 1960s filtertip cigarettes conferred any protection against coronary heart disease (or other adverse health consequences of smoking) remains equivocal.

Filtertip cigarettes, however, have evolved further since the 1960s and early 1970s. Current cigarettes are diluted by porous materials and perforations in the filters. Smokers compensate for the air dilution by smoking each cigarette more intensively and, possibly, by blocking the perforations. Moreover, the newest cigarettes contain additives, such as artificial tobacco substitutes and flavoring extracts, whose identity, chemical composition, and health effects are as yet unknown.

Accordingly, who cuts down on cigarettes, who quits, and who fails to start are critical questions in assessing the quantitative effect of a cigarette tax increase on the health of the population. That an increase in price appears to reduce the proportion of smokers is likely to figure prominently in such an analysis.

Based upon the findings of epidemiological studies conducted during the 1950s, 1960s, and 1970s, I estimate that out of a cohort of 100 males who become regular cigarette smokers in their teens, about 11 will not survive to age sixty-five because of their cigarette smoking. For a comparable cohort of 100 women, about 7 will die before age sixty-five, who would have otherwise survived to that age. For males and females combined, about 9 percent will not survive to age sixty-five because of their smoking. If these estimates apply to current smokers, and if increased taxes prevented 600,000 teenagers from starting to smoke, then 54,000 additional teenagers will reach age sixty-five. Computation of the mortality consequences for regular smokers who quit smoking will depend upon the age distribution of those who quit. Roughly speaking, even if the effect of quitting were only one fourth that of not smoking at all, then I obtain an additional 45,000 survivors to age sixty-five years. Altogether, this would imply that about 100,000 additional persons will live to age sixty-five as a result of price-induced declines in cigarette use.

Although there was indeed a period when the real price of cigarettes fell (Figure 1), we have no clear evidence that the hypothesized effect of a price increase is reversible. Thus, although prices fell during 1971–1981, the proportion of cigarette smokers did not rise (Table 4). It is conceivable that, if real price had not fallen, the declines in the prevalence of cigarette use might have accelerated during 1971–1981. Still, if increased prices were sustained for a sufficiently long period, and if one effect of such price increases were to deter teenagers from smoking, then a subsequent fall in price may not induce them to start smoking. The great fraction of persons now starting to smoke cigarettes do so while teenagers. Sustained, irreversible declines in cigarette use would have very different health consequences than temporary changes due to short-term price fluctuations.

4. Unanswered Questions

This paper has left unanswered a number of questions that merit further research.

My conclusion that manufacturers' price increases were not matched by cost increases is based on incomplete data. It would be appropriate to assess more carefully manufacturers' profit margins by domestic tobacco lines of business. It would be further desirable to ascertain whether the gains from cigarette price increases figured in other nontobacco corporate acquisitions made by the manufacturers.

I noted that manufacturers began to introduce generic and discount cigarettes in substantial numbers beginning in 1982. Although I attempted to take account of the presence of such discount brands in my computations of manufacturers' wholesale prices, I said nothing about their role in corporate pricing strategy. With respect to the analysis of variations in price sensitivity across consumers, it would be interesting to ascertain what types of consumers demand such brands.

I mentioned that changes in the type of cigarette consumed may affect the costs of production. I also discussed how future changes in cigarette composition may affect the health consequences of current price changes. However, I said little about who consumes such cigarettes. Nor did I ask whether the introduction of "low tar" brands has affected consumers' sensitivity to price.

I did not ask how long manufacturers' price increases might persist. If the increase in the federal excise tax had been originally enacted as permanent, then I speculate that most of the price increase would have been realized by the end of 1984. However, the fact that the tax was supposed to sunset in October 1985 may have moved manufacturers to persist in price increases. I examined data on wholesale prices only up to June 1986. One wonders what will be the pattern of manufacturers' prices now that the tax increase has been made permanent.

I focused on manufacturers' price increases, but I sidestepped the fact that wholesalers' and retailers' markups also increased. I am not sure whether such intermediate sellers also took advantage of the confusion surrounding the tax increase, or whether their markups are determined by other rules, such as state fair-trade laws.

I concluded that rising prices were probably responsible for most of the decline in cigarette consumption during the 1980s. Such a finding does not by itself imply that public and private sector education has had no effect. One can only conclude that the net effects of such informational efforts may be canceled by other factors, including promotional activities of manufacturers.

If increases in cigarette prices deter teenagers from starting, then the current period of sustained real price increases may have substantial long-term effects on the population of cigarette smokers. It would be of interest to know whether American cigarette manufacturers, in opting for such price increases, considered a balancing of these potential long-term losses against short-run profit gains. That would, of course, require predictions about the future path of the American cigarette industry, which I shall resist.

REFERENCES

Baltagi, B. H., and D. Levin. 1986. Estimating dynamic demand for cigarettes using panel data: The effects of bootlegging, taxation and advertising reconsidered. *Review of Economics and Statistics* 68: 148–55.

Barzel, Y. 1976. An alternative approach to the analysis of taxation. *Journal of Political Economy* 84: 1177–97.

Bishop, J. A., and J. H. Yoo. 1985. "Health scare," excise taxes and advertising ban in cigarette demand and supply. *Southern Economic Journal* 52: 402–11.

Bulow, J. I., and P. Pfleiderer. 1983. A note on the effect of cost changes on prices. *Journal of Political Economy* 91: 182–85.

Chappell, V. G. 1985. The burden of tobacco taxes by income class. *Tobacco International* (July 26): 98–102.

Doll, R., and R. Peto. 1978. Cigarette smoking and bronchial carcinoma. Dose and time relationships among regular smokers and lifelong non-smokers. *Journal of Epidemiology and Community Health* 32: 303–13.

Gray, H. P., and I. Walter. 1986. The economic contribution of the tobacco industry. In *Smoking and society. Toward a more balanced assessment*, ed. R. Tollison, chap. 9. Lexington, Mass.: D.C. Heath.

Hamilton, J. L. 1974. The demand for cigarettes: Advertising, the health scare, and the cigarette advertising ban. *Review of Economics and Statistics* 54: 401–11.

Harris, J. E. 1979. Cigarette smoking in the United States, 1950–1978. In *Smoking and health. A report of the Surgeon General*, A-1–A-29. DHEW Publication No. (PHS) 79-50066. Washington, D.C.: U.S. Government Printing Office.

———. 1980a. Taxing tar and nicotine. *American Economic Review* 70: 300–11.

———. 1980b. Patterns of cigarette smoking. In *The health consequences of smoking* for women. *A report of the Surgeon General,* 15–42, Washington, D.C.: U.S. Government Printing Office.

———. 1982. Increasing the federal excise tax on cigarettes. *Journal of Health Economics* 1: 117–20.

———. 1983. Cigarette smoking among successive birth cohorts of men and women in the United States during 1900–80. *Journal of the National Cancer Institute* 71: 473–79.

———. 1986. On the fairness of cigarette excise taxation. In *The cigarette excise tax, April 17, 1985.* Cambridge: Harvard University Institute for the Study of Smoking Behavior and Policy, Conference Series.

Ippolito, R. A., D. R. Murphy, and D. Sant. 1979. Consumer responses to cigarette health information. Bureau of Economics Staff Report. Washington, D.C.: Federal Trade Commission.

Lewit, E. M., and D. Coate. 1982. The potential for using excise taxes to reduce smoking. *Journal of Health Economics* 1: 121–46.

Lewit, E. M., D. Coate, and M. Grossman. 1981. The effects of government regulation on teenage smoking. *Journal of Law and Economics* 24: 545–69.

Moody's Investor's Service. 1986. *Moody's industrial manual.* New York.

Nicholls, W. H. 1949. The tobacco case of 1946. *American Economic Review Papers and Proceedings* 39: 284–96.

Porter, R. H. 1986. The impact of government policy on the U.S. cigarette industry. In *Empirical approaches to consumer protection economics,* eds. P. M. Ippolito and D. T. Scheffman, 447–81. Bureau of Economics Conference Volume. Washington, D.C.: Federal Trade Commission.

Rotemberg, J. J., and G. Saloner. 1986. A supergame-theoretic model of price wars during booms. *American Economic Review* 76: 390–407.

Schneider, L., B. Klein, and K. M. Murphy. 1981. Government regulation of cigarette health information. *Journal of Law and Economics* 24: 575–612.

Shughart, W. F. II, and J. M. Savarese. 1986. The incidence of taxes on tobacco. In *Smoking and society. Toward a more balanced assessment,* ed. R. Tollison, chap. 11. Lexington, Mass.: D.C. Heath.

Sullivan, D. 1985. Testing hypotheses about firm behavior in the cigarette industry. *Journal of Political Economy* 91: 586–98.

Sumner, D. A. 1981. Measurement of monopoly behavior: An application to the cigarette industry. *Journal of Political Economy* 89: 1010–19.

Toder, E. J. 1986. Issues in the taxation of cigarettes. In *The cigarette excise tax, April 17, 1985.* Cambridge: Harvard University Institute for the Study of Smoking Behavior and Policy, Conference Series.

U.S. Department of Agriculture, Economic Research Service. *Tobacco situation and outlook reports.* Washington, D.C., various issues.

U.S. Department of Health and Human Services. 1984. *The health consequences of smoking: Cardiovascular disease. A report of the Surgeon General.* DHHS Publication Number (PHS) 84-50204. Washington, D.C.: U.S. Government Printing Office.

U.S. Department of Treasury. *Treasury bulletin.* Washington, D.C., various issues.

U.S. Federal Trade Commission. 1984. Report to Congress pursuant to the federal cigarette labelling and advertising act, for the year 1981. Washington, D.C.: U.S. Federal Trade Commission.

———. 1986. Report to Congress pursuant to the federal cigarette labelling and advertising act, for the year 1984. Washington, D.C.: U.S. Federal Trade Commission.

U.S. National Center for Health Statistics. 1985. *Health United States 1984.* DHHS Publication Number (PHS) 85-1232. Washington, D.C.: U.S. Government Printing Office.

————. 1986. Health promotion and disease prevention. Provisional data from the National Health Interview Survey: United States, January–June 1985. *Advance Data from Vital and Health Statistics* No. 119, May 14.

Warner, K. E. 1986. Consumption impacts of a change in the federal cigarette excise tax. In *The cigarette excise tax, April 17, 1985.* Cambridge: Harvard University Institute for the Study of Smoking Behavior and Policy, Conference Series.

B. Douglas Bernheim

Stanford University and NBER

Does the Estate Tax Raise Revenue?

1. Introduction

Proponents of tranfer taxation argue that well-designed levies on estates and gifts serve two primary objectives. First, such taxes may promote an equitable distribution of economic resources by breaking up large concentrations of wealth. Yet many commentators have noted that common estate-planning techniques allow wealthy individuals to transfer vast fortunes while paying little or no tax (see, e.g., Cooper (1979)). Accordingly, it is possible that this first objective is served only in cases where individuals have little or no desire to avoid taxation. Second, transfer taxes raise revenue. In practice, levies on gifts and estates have raised roughly $6 billion per year over the last five years. This sum is certainly substantial, but one should bear in mind that it represents less than 1 percent of all federal revenues for the same period, despite the imposition of high statutory marginal tax rates. One might therefore be inclined to conclude that transfer taxation achieves the second objective with perhaps a modicum of success.

Unfortunately, this conclusion is premature. To measure the true revenues associated with transfer taxation, one must determine the net incremental contribution that these taxes make to total federal revenues, or, to put it another way, one must estimate the amount by which total revenues would decline if these taxes were eliminated. This figure may bear very little relation to measures of collected revenue reported by the government. In particular, many of the same estate-planning techniques that allow wealthy individuals to escape transfer taxation also have important income tax implications. Thus, elimination of transfer taxes might significantly affect income tax revenues.

This work was supported in part by the National Science Foundation through Grant No. SES8607630.

In this paper, I argue that, as a consequence of behavioral responses to estate taxation, a substantial amount of capital income is taxed at lower marginal rates under the personal income tax. I emphasize two major channels through which this occurs. First, estate planners agree that perhaps the best method of avoiding estate taxes is to make substantial intra vivos gifts, and to make them as early in life as possible. Typically, wealthy individuals can do this in ways that minimize or entirely eliminate gift tax liabilities. The net effect is to transfer wealth, typically from parents to children, during a period of life in which children tend to pay lower marginal rates under the personal income tax. Although differences between marginal income tax rates alone create incentives for wealthy individuals to make intra vivos gifts,[1] the estate tax adds to this incentive, presumably generating larger transfers. The government effectively forgoes a portion of its tax claim on incrementally transferred assets. Second, since charitable bequests are deductible from gross estate for tax purposes, the estate tax creates a substantial incentive to make such contributions. Even though one might well deem this a desirable outcome, it is important to recognize that it too has important consequences for the income tax. In this case, resources are transferred from individuals with positive marginal tax rates to tax-exempt institutions. As a result, the government forgoes its entire claim on the transferred assets.

Unfortunately, it is extremely difficult to measure these effects precisely. The most important obstacle is the availability of extensive financial data on a sample drawn from the wealthiest 5 percent of the population. Although most of this information is, in principle, contained in federal personal income, estate, and gift tax returns, the IRS is reluctant to release such information for fear of violating the confidentiality of wealthy taxpayers. Even if this data became available, the measurement of intra vivos transfers (which are often well disguised) would pose severe conceptual difficulties. My strategy in this paper is to estimate true revenues on the basis of the best available evidence. Since this evidence is admittedly sketchy, it is appropriate to think of my calculations as suggestive rather than precise.

Two major conclusions emerge from this study. First, the indirect effects of estate taxation on federal personal income tax revenue are potentially of the same order of magnitude as the reported revenue collected by this tax. Thus, these reported figures may lead one quite far astray.

---

1. For this reason, changes in the taxation of personal income affect estate tax revenues, just as estate taxation affects income tax revenues. We return to this point in section 6.

Second, available evidence suggests that, historically, true revenues associated with estate taxation may well have been near zero, or even negative. Recent tax reforms that reduce the progressivity of federal personal income tax rates only partially vitiate this conclusion. Far from "backing up" the income tax as some have claimed, the estate tax may actually generate a rise in income tax avoidance activities sufficient to offset revenue collected through estate levies.

This paper is organized as follows. In section 2, I briefly review the history of federal estate and gift taxes, paying special attention to provisions that play prominent roles in the following analysis. I elaborate upon the incentive effects of estate taxation in section 3, and present evidence documenting significant behaviorial adjustments to changes in the tax code in section 4. Section 5 contains estimates of net revenue raised through estate taxation, which are adjusted to account for the behavioral responses discussed in sections 3 and 4. In section 6, I turn my attention to several additional considerations, some of which introduce potentially countervailing forces. Special attention is given to various provisions of the Tax Reform Act of 1986 (TRA). Section 7 contains conclusions.

2. A Brief History of Federal Estate and Gift Taxation

The modern estate tax has been in effect since 1916. The original legislation provided for a $50,000 exemption, with progressive marginal tax rates rising from 1 percent to 10 percent for estates over $10 million. The gift tax was instituted in 1924. Rates ranged from 1 percent to 25 percent, matching estate tax rates in the same year. Donors were provided with a $50,000 exemption, plus a $5,000 annual exclusion per donee. As of 1932, gift tax rates were reduced relative to estate tax rates and remained 25 percent lower than estate rates through 1976.

From 1943 to 1976, the basic provisions of federal estate and gift taxes remained essentially unchanged. The law provided for a $60,000 estate tax exemption, with progressive rates ranging from 3 percent to 77 percent. The gift tax exemption was fixed at $30,000, with a $3,000 annual exclusion per donee. Decedents were allowed to bequeath one half of their gross estates to their spouses tax free (the marital deduction), and all charitable bequests were deductible. In addition, recipients of bequests were allowed to step up the basis on all assets for purposes of capital gains taxation to the fair-market value of those assets at the time of their benefactor's death. A step-up of basis was not allowed for assets transferred by gift.

Congress significantly altered the structure of federal transfer taxes in the TRA of 1976. Most importantly, this act provided for unification of estate and gift taxes. Since 1976, all cognizable transfers have been taxed jointly under the same progressive schedule, which originally includes a maximum rate of 70 percent. Lifetime giving is still slightly favored because the gift tax is imposed only on the net transfer, whereas the estate tax base also includes amounts used to pay the tax. The act also established a unified credit that provided tax relief equivalent to a $60,000 exemption, but which was designed to rise in steps over a period of years. The $3,000 yearly gift tax exclusion was retained, and the marital deduction was liberalized, so decedents could transfer the maximum of $250,000 and 50 percent of gross estate tax free. Finally, Congress removed the step-up of basis at death, but this provision was later repealed.

The Economic Recovery Tax Act of 1981 (ERTA) embraced four major changes to this system of transfer taxation. First, the unified credit was increased in steps to a maximum of $192,800 in 1987 (equivalent to a $600,000 exemption). Second, the maximum marginal tax rate was decreased in steps from 70 to 50 percent. Third, all limits on the marital deduction were removed. Finally, the annual gift tax exclusion was raised to $10,000.

3. Incentive Effects of Estate Taxation

In this section, I argue that the federal estate tax has generated strong incentives for individuals to transfer large amounts of accumulated wealth to their intended heirs prior to death, and to do so as early in life as possible. Furthermore, I note that the deductibility of charitable bequests enhances the attractiveness of leaving a portion of one's estate to charity. In subsequent sections, I document the effects of these incentives on behavior and compute the attendant impact on federal personal income tax revenues.

3.1 INTRA VIVOS GIFTS

Before 1977, the federal tax system treated gifts more favorably than bequests. Despite the unification of gift and estate taxes in the TRA of 1976, virtually all estate planners still recommend a plan of systematic lifetime giving as perhaps the most important method of transfer tax avoidance (see Brosterman (1977), Kess and Westlin (1982), Esperti and Peterson (1983), Clay (1982), and Cooper (1979)). Cooper argues that

The first major goal of good estate planning is to freeze the size of a client's estate at its current level and divert future growth to the natural objects of the client's bounty. . . . it is far easier to divert future growth than it is to disgorge wealth

already accumulated, and good estate planning attempts to get estate-freezing action into operation as soon as possible *[emphasis added] so as to cut off wealth accumulation before it becomes a more serious planning problem.*

In practice, there are many ways to accomplish this while simultaneously minimizing or entirely avoiding gift tax liability. Since these planning techniques have been reviewed at length elsewhere, I will provide only a brief summary of the major strategies.

3.1.1. Undisguised gifts   Since a substantial amount of gifts is entirely exempt from taxation, a simple plan of undisguised lifetime giving is, for the majority of families, the most effective estate planning tool. By splitting gifts, a married couple can now transfer $20,000 ($6,000 prior to 1982) per year to each intended heir without incurring any gift tax liability whatsoever. Thus, a couple with two children could divest itself of $1 million over a twenty-five year period simply by taking advantage of the gift tax exclusion. If the couple is willing to contemplate gifts to grandchildren or to spouses of children or grandchildren, the potential for transfer tax avoidance grows enormously.

It is, however, essential to begin taking advantage of the gift tax exclusion as early as possible. For one thing, the timing of each individual's death is uncertain, and all assets remaining in his possession at the time of his death are taxable as part of his estate. In addition, the exemption is not cumulative, so failure to take advantage of it in any particular year implies that one opportunity to make tax-free transfers has been lost forever. This consideration may be quite important for very wealthy individuals who, despite programs of systematic lifetime giving, still expect to die with substantial estates.

The TRA of 1976 also provides substantial unified credits against estate and gift tax liabilities. At first, it might appear as though this provision treats gifts and bequests neutrally. However, this impression is erroneous. As long as donors plan to exhaust the credit completely, its value is inversely related to the date at which they choose to take it. This principle is easily demonstrated. For simplicity, assume that the credit is fixed at its 1987 level of $192,800 so that it corresponds to an exemption of $600,000. Consider a wealthy man who, among other things, owns a piece of property worth $600,000. He may transfer the entire parcel to his heirs immediately without incurring any tax liability. Upon his eventual demise, his estate will pay taxes only on the residual assets. If, on the other hand, he holds the property until his death, it will ordinarily escalate in value. Suppose he dies ten years later and the property is then worth $1 million. The first $600,000 would be exempt. However, his estate would then pay taxes not only on the residual assets but also on the $400,000 gain.[2] At current rates, this would imply an incremental estate tax liability of between $150,000 and $200,000.

3.1.2. Diversion of Profitable Investment Opportunities Perhaps the most common and informal estate planning activity entails the diversion of profitable investment opportunities to one's intended heirs. Parents can provide valuable information and advice concerning potential investments without incurring gift tax liability. In many cases, parents devote great effort to locating and arranging profitable business deals and then bring their children in as coinvestors. Such diversions do not generate any incremental tax liabilities, even though their success may depend upon expert services supplied by the parent. If children lack the necessary capital, parents can lend it to them. As long as these loans are made at prevailing rates of interest and observe arms-length regulations, no gift tax liability is incurred even if the child would have been unable to obtain a similar loan from a third party. Alternatively, parents can help their children to obtain a loan at favorable rates by guaranteeing repayment, without risk of transfer taxation. Finally, parents can provide assurances that, should the deal fail, they will pick up the loss. In the event a loss actually occurs, parents will be compelled to pay gift tax on the associated transfer. However, from the point of view of a risk-averse child, the parents' guarantee amounts to an insurance policy, the value of which exceeds their expected loss.

For parents who own large portions of businesses or closely held corporations, additional opportunities for diversions arise. In many cases, parents can shift profitable activities from their primary business to a separate partnership or enterprise owned partially or completely by their children. Parents may also bring their children into a family partnership as silent partners, thereby diverting a share of the earnings and appreciation from their business. To accomplish this while minimizing taxable transfers, they must arrange the partnership as early as possible.

3.1.3 Sophisticated Estate Tax Avoidance Various sophisticated estate-planning techniques allow wealthy individuals to transfer resources intra vivos in ways that escape notice under the gift tax. Important techniques are the use of preferred stock recapitalizations in closely held firms, installment sales, and life insurance.

2. In general, only part of this gain will be due to inflation. Thus, the argument remains valid even if the credit is indexed.

In a preferred stock recapitalization, parents cancel outstanding common stock and issue in its place a combination of preferred and common stocks. They distribute the preferred stock primarily to themselves (or other current owners), the common stock primarily to their children (or other intended heirs). If desired, this can be accomplished without transferring significant control over the corporation to the children. By selecting an appropriate dividend entitlement for the preferred stock, the parent can reduce the value of the common stock to a negligible level, reflecting only the speculative growth potential of the corporation. In this way, parents entirely avoid the gift tax but succeed in transferring all future corporate growth, brought about in part by their own expertise and effort, to their children. One difficulty is that parents may be forced to accept a high level of taxable personal income from the preferred stock. Nevertheless, in many cases such income is desirable and estate planners tend to recommend the recapitalization.

Installment sales are frequently used to transfer real property. Parents sell this property to their children while simultaneously providing financing. They then typically forgive interest payments as they come due. In some cases, they use the property for business activities and lease it back from the children. Rental payments then partially offset interest payments, and the remaining interest is typically forgiven. All forgiven interest is potentially taxable as a gift. The primary advantage of the installment sale is that parents can transfer all accumulation on the entire parcel immediately, despite the fact that the bulk of actual gifts (forgiven interest payments) will not be made for many years. In addition, when parents use the property for business activities, they may be able to develop it with the ultimate benefit eventually accruing free of tax to their children. Finally, it is even possible to provide, as part of the terms of the original sale, that the installment payments will terminate upon the parents' death, without drawing the unpaid portion into the parents' estate. The primary disadvantage of the installment sale is that it forces parents to realize a capital gain. However, they can defer realization by using balloon payments. Furthermore, upon the parents' demise, it appears possible to largely eliminate capital gains obligations on the remaining portion.

Life insurance provides a particularly attractive estate planning tool for highly paid executives. It is quite common for corporations (particularly those closely held) to provide their executives with large amounts of life insurance as a fringe benefit. An executive may assign ownership in this insurance to prospective heirs, thereby excluding it from the estate. Although premiums over a certain threshold are taxable to the executive under the personal income tax, assignment of ownership in such a policy to heirs is apparently not cognizable as a gift. As a result, this scheme completely avoids transfer taxes. Since this arrangement can be used for ordinary life insurance as well as group term insurance, the net effect can be to transfer resources into an accumulating whole life policy. Since investment income accruing to policyholders within life insurance companies is tax exempt, the government thereby forgoes its entire claim on the transferred assets until the executive's death.

3.1.4 Evasion   Many families presumably engage in simple gift tax evasion. It is certainly possible for individuals to make substantial gifts in forms that are difficult, if not impossible, for the IRS to trace. Outright gifts of cash and durable goods (clothes, furniture, appliances) fall into this category.

Each of these techniques for avoiding estate and gift taxes has the ultimate effect of transferring resources from parent to child at a relatively early date. Indeed, in most cases, effective planning requires these transfers to be made as early as possible. To the extent children face significantly lower marginal rates under the personal income, significant losses of tax revenue may result.

It is important to bear in mind that wealthy individuals are not solely motivated by the desire to minimize taxes. Indeed, estate planners emphasize that this goal often conflicts with other legitimate concerns, such as retaining control over one's assets, maintaining one's desired standard of living, and providing one's children with appropriate incentives. Proper estate planning balances the costs and benefits of tax avoidance at the margin. For this very reason, we would expect changes in the tax treatment of gifts and bequests to affect intra vivos transfers significantly.

3.2 CHARITABLE BEQUESTS

Incentives for charitable giving arise directly from the deductibility of such bequests for estate tax purposes. If, for example, an individual faces a marginal estate tax rate of 50 percent, she can by forgoing $0.50 of bequests to her heirs provide $1 to charity. The effective price of contributing $1 to charity is therefore only $0.50 (in general, this price is $(1 − t)$, where t is the testator's marginal estate tax rate). Sophisticated estate planners may also recommend the use of front-end trusts, which provide that the income from an estate be used for charitable purposes over some specified period, after which all assets are returned to the decedent's heirs. Such an arrangement can virtually eliminate all estate taxes while preserving substantial value for one's descendants.

4. Behavioral Evidence

The estate tax creates strong incentive for wealthy individuals to make intra vivos gifts and charitable bequests; however, this does not necessarily imply that these tax incentives have a significant effect on behavior. Accordingly, I now present empirical evidence concerning actual behavioral responses. As we shall see, the evidence strongly supports the view that these responses are extremely large.

4.1 INTRA VIVOS TRANSFERS

Unfortunately, data on gifts are virtually impossible to obtain, in part because they are often disguised as other sorts of transactions (recall the discussion in section 3). Although one can obtain some information on trusts from IRS fiduciary income tax data, it is not possible to distinguish between the formation of revocable and irrevocable trusts. A revocable trust is not a consummated gift and is therefore treated as part of the donor's assets for tax purposes. As a result, this data is uninformative.

One can, nevertheless, document the sensitivity of intra vivos transfers to tax code provisions indirectly. Note in particular that the choice between making a gift or a bequest is essentially one of timing. Parents can transfer wealth to their children immediately or hang on to it for some time, eventually making the same transfer upon death. This decision is therefore closely related to the choice of whether to bequeath assets to one's spouse or directly to one's ultimate heirs. In this case, the couple can choose to transfer wealth to its children immediately upon the death of the first spouse, or hang on to it and eventually make the same transfer upon the death of the second spouse.[3] Again, the issue is simply one of timing. However, unlike intra vivos transfers, ample information is available concerning bequests to spouses. Furthermore, ERTA fundamentally changed the tax treatment of spousal bequests as of 1982 by eliminating all limitations on the marital deduction. In addition, the reduction of tax rates in 1977 somewhat diminished the penalty associated with double taxation of wealth passed first to one's spouse and eventually to one's ultimate heirs. Finally, the reduction of maximum tax rates in 1982 somewhat vitiated the importance of planning for very wealthy decedents to split transfers to children or other ultimate heirs evenly between spouses' estates. Thus, by examining trends in spousal bequests over the last ten years or so, one can infer the importance of

---

3. One obvious difference is that an individual might not be sure that his or her spouse would make the same bequests later on that he or she would have made. However, it is possible to overcome this difficulty through the use of a trust.

estate tax provisions in determining the timing of transfers to ultimate heirs.[4]

To measure behavioral responses to changes in the tax code, I will compare IRS statistics on bequests to spouses from 1977 and 1983 returns. Most returns filed in any year concern the estates of individuals who died in the previous year. Thus, the 1977 returns primarily contain estates treated under 1976 law (pre-TRA of 1976), and the 1983 returns consist primarily of estates taxed under ERTA.

Since the filing requirement changed dramatically between 1976 and 1982 (from $60,000 to $225,000), the 1977 and 1983 returns reflect radically different samples. In addition, data are only available on 1983 returns for which the gross estate exceeded $300,000. To restore comparability, one must restrict attention to 1977 returns on which reported gross estate is sufficiently large. In particular, the $300,000 threshold is, adjusting for inflation, roughly equivalent to $180,000 in 1976. Unfortunately, the IRS is no longer willing to release data on individual returns, so it is necessary to employ aggregated statistics. The IRS does, however, report sample averages for these data, grouped by size of gross estate. Thus, it is possible to restrict attention to 1977 returns on which the gross estate exceeded $150,000 or $200,000. In practice, we consider all estates exceeding a $200,000 threshold, in part because this is closer to $180,000, and in part because this selection criterion produces a sample of 59,553 returns. Given their similar sizes, there is every reason to believe that

4. Unfortunately, this period also witnessed the adoption of significant income tax reforms (under ERTA). Thus, changes in gift and bequest behavior may reflect a combination of effects (see footnote 1). One would not, however, expect income tax provisions to significantly affect the fraction of bequests left to spouses, because after the testator's death, all primary heirs (spouses and children) will ordinarily pay similar high-bracket marginal personal income tax rates. In addition, the limitation of the marital deduction was undoubtedly the single most important tax-related determinant of spousal bequests, and its elimination probably swamped all other effects. For these reasons, data on spousal bequests may actually be preferable to data on intra vivos transfers.

Table 1   A COMPARISON OF 1977 AND 1983 ESTATE TAX RETURNS

	1977 Returns	*1983 Returns*
Minimum gross estate in sample	$200,000	$300,000
Percent gross estates of married decedents left to spouses	47.7	59.4
Percent married decedents claiming marital deduction	89.8	95.3
Percent gross estates of all decedents left to charity	8.09	5.05

these two samples reflect nearly identical segments of the population. I should mention, however, that the use of $150,000 (rather than $200,000) as a selection criterion would not significantly alter my conclusions.

Comparison of statistics for these samples reveals the following pattern (see Table 1). For returns filed in 1977, married individuals left $0.477 out of every dollar to their spouses. For returns filed in 1983, this figure climbed to $0.594 on the dollar, a net increase of 24.5 percent.[5]

Although this response is enormous, one might well wonder why it was not even more pronounced. After all, ERTA allows individuals to transfer unlimited resources to their spouses absolutely tax free. There are at least three explanations. First, individuals may adjust their wills somewhat slowly in response to changes in estate tax provisions. Indeed, one should recall that 1982 was the first year in which decedents were allowed an unlimited marital deduction; this deduction may have been used to an even greater extent in subsequent years. Second, many decedents exhausted the benefit of the marital deduction by driving their estate taxes to zero. Indeed, 78.6 percent of those claiming the marital deduction paid no tax. Overall, the effective tax rate on married decedents was a mere 4.7 percent, as compared to 17.5 percent for the rest of the sample. Third, even with an unlimited marital deduction, it is not always optimal to bequeath all assets to a surviving spouse, since this strategy could lead to a large estate tax liability upon the death of the second spouse.

A comparison of 1977 and 1983 returns also reveals an increase in the frequency with which individuals claimed the marital deduction (refer again to Table 1). For the 1977 returns, 102 out of every 1,000 married decedents failed to claim this deduction. By 1983, this figure had fallen to 47 out of every 1,000 married decedents, a decline of 53.9 percent. One cannot attribute this trend to the elimination of limitations on the marital deduction under ERTA, since those not claiming the deduction were not constrained by these limitations. Rather, this trend is a direct reflection of the decline in estate tax rates, which reduce the penalty associated with transferring wealth first to one's surviving spouse, and subsequently, upon the spouse's death, to one's heirs.

Overall, this evidence confirms the view that the timing of transfers to one's ultimate heirs is extremely sensitive to estate tax provisions. Accordingly, there is a strong presumption that intra vivos gifts exhibit a similar sensitivity.

5. After subtracting liabilities such as funeral and administrative expenses, debts and mortgages, one finds that bequests to other heirs increased by roughly the same proportion.

4.2 CHARITABLE BEQUESTS

Previous investigators have directly estimated the effect of estate tax provisions on charitable bequests (see, e.g., McNees (1973), Feldstein (1977), Boskin (1976), Barthold and Plotnick (1983), and Clotfelter (1984)). In general, these estimates suggest that the behavioral response is extremely large. For example, Clotfelter found that a 1 percent rise in the effective price of charitable bequests (see section 3.2) would cause such bequests to decline by roughly 1 percent, and perhaps by as much as 1.5 percent. Clotfelter used his estimates to simulate the effect of ERTA on charitable giving. On the basis of his calculations, he predicted that ERTA would depress charitable bequests by 34 percent to 52 percent.

In this instance, economists have the rare opportunity to determine the accuracy of a prediction based upon econometric estimates of behavioral responses by examining actual responses pursuant to a policy change. Unfortunately, the IRS has not made any data on estate tax returns available for any year between 1977 and 1983. Thus, of necessity, the data samples used here span both the 1976 and 1981 tax reforms. Accordingly, any changes in behavior reflect responses to both acts. On the other hand, ERTA was phased in over several years, so its full effect was not felt in 1982. These two factors roughly offset each other, so that one can still obtain a feel for the accuracy of Clotfelter's predictions by comparing charitable bequests across two samples.

Specifically, we find that for 1977 returns, decedents left $0.0809 out of every dollar to charity. By 1983, this figure had fallen to $0.0505 on the dollar (see Table 1). The magnitude of this decline (37.6 percent) is roughly in line with the low end of the range of possible responses predicted by Clotfelter. Since, once again, individuals may adjust their wills slowly in response to changes in estate tax provisions, the observed response should be thought of as a lower bound. Actual experience therefore provides striking confirmation of ex ante econometric forecasts.

Having established that estate taxation not only creates incentives for intra vivos giving and charitable bequests but also that these incentives have an enormous impact on behavior, we now consider the implications for personal income tax revenues.

5. True Estate Tax Revenues

I have argued in previous sections that reported estate tax revenue figures may be quite misleading. To calculate true revenues, one must net out indirect effects. As a first step, it is essential to determine proper methods for measuring revenues. When an individual holds an asset, the government effectively owns some claim on that asset. However, the value of the government's claim depends in a fairly complex way upon the individual's marginal tax rate and upon his or her behavior.

Consider, for example, the effect of transferring a consol worth $1 from one taxpayer to another. Suppose that the interest rate is 10 percent, so the consol pays $0.10 each year. Taxpayer A is now, and always will be, in the 50 percent marginal tax bracket. Furthermore, suppose that A would hold the consol indefinitely, consuming all of the after-tax income it produces. If A owns the consol, then the government has a claim on a stream of $0.05 payments in every subsequent year. Taxpayer B is now, and always will be, in the 25 percent marginal tax bracket. Furthermore, B would also hold the consol indefinitely, consuming exactly its after-tax proceeds. If B owns the consol, then the government has a claim on a stream of $0.025 payments in every subsequent year.

To compare these streams with measures of current revenues, one must calculate present values. The appropriate discount rate for the government is the after-tax rate of return for some average government bondholder (see Feldstein (1974)). Suppose that this average bondholder is in the 40 percent tax bracket. Then if A owns the consol, the value of the government's claim is $0.833, whereas if B holds the consol, the value of this claim falls to $0.417. Accordingly, if some policy induces A to give B the consol, the government loses $0.417.

I remarked earlier that the value of the government's claim depends not only upon the individual's marginal tax rate but also upon his or her behavior. To illustrate, suppose that A and B would, if given the consol, sell it immediately (before receiving any income) to C and consume all the proceeds. Then any policy that induces A to give the consol to B obviously has no income tax implications, despite differences in the marginal tax rates of these individuals. This hypothetical case raises a general point: as taxpayers' marginal propensities to consume their resources rise, the value of the government's claim on their wealth falls. Since investments produce taxable income, reinvestment is tantamount to transferring a portion of the after-tax claim to the government. If, as one would expect, wealthy individuals have higher propensities to reinvest, then transfers of assets from high- to low-bracket taxpayers will have an even greater impact on income tax revenues than indicated by the preceding hypothetical calculation.

Although I have cast this discussion in terms of a consol, the same reasoning applies equally well to all coupon bonds (by rolling these over, one can effectively produce a consol). Since capital gains have always received special treatment under the tax law, analogous calculations for stocks and real property are a bit more complex. One must specify the

fraction of earnings paid out as current income (dividends or rent) and
the frequency with which individuals turn over assets, in addition to
marginal tax rates and propensities to consume. Details of all such computations appear in the Appendix.

Throughout the following analysis, I employ the revenue valuation
formulas derived in the Appendix. I assume a nominal interest rate of
8 percent. In addition, I take the dividend/earning ratio on stocks to be
0.5. Finally, I assume that investors turn over about 10 percent of their
assets each year. This implies that corporate shares are held on average
for 10 years (see King (1977)). I make no special calculations for real estate holdings, but treat them analogously to stock.

5.1 INTRA VIVOS TRANSFERS

I now turn to the problem of estimating the indirect revenue effects of
induced intra vivos transfers. The first task is to measure the average
ratio of gifts to bequests in a given year. I infer this ratio by combining
several available figures. Kotlikoff and Summers (1981) estimated that in
1974 total intra vivos transfers were approximated 1.56 times the size of
intergenerational bequests.[6] Unpublished data collected by Paul Menchik and Martin David from 1967 estate tax records and reported by
Kotlikoff and Summers allow us to determine the fraction of gross estates bequeathed across generations by sex and marital status of the decedent. Combining the Menchik–David figures with estate tax data on
the distribution of gross estates over the same categories of decedents, I
find that approximately $0.338 out of every dollar of gross estates is be-
queathed across generations. Thus, for every dollar of reported bequests, individuals concurrently transfer approximately $0.527 (= 1.56 ×
$0.338) intra vivos. One can use this figure to estimate the likely mag-
nitude of gifts in any desired year. For example, in 1983 the total value
of all gross estates exceeding $300,000 was $50.4 billion. Accordingly,
surviving individuals of similar economic status (age adjusted) probably transferred about $26.5 billion (= 0.527 × 50.4 billion) intra vivos
in 1983.[7]

6. Specifically, they estimated that transfers across generations totaled about $70 billion,
   and they attributed approximately 60.9 percent of this to intra vivos transfers. Intra
   vivos transfers include life insurance policies in which the incidents of ownership have
   been transferred to the beneficiary and which are therefore excluded from gross estate.
7. One could question this calculation on several grounds. First, wealthy individuals have
   more incentive to engage in estate planning and therefore probably make a larger fraction of their transfers intra vivos than do average individuals. For this reason, the calculation probably understates the true magnitude of such transfers. Second, a number
   of significant tax reforms took place between 1974 (the year for which Kotlikoff and
   Summers made their calculations) and 1983. These reforms included (i) the unification of

Not all of this is attributable to the estate tax. However, it seems reasonable to conclude on the basis of the evidence presented in section 4 that elimination of estate levies would have reduced this number by at least 25 percent. I have already argued that this evidence probably understates the true behavioral response for a variety of reasons. Indeed, estate planners often emphasize that lifetime gifts have various adverse nontax consequences, including loss of control over resources and premature enrichment of one's children, and they often recommend that individuals consider such transfers only if the tax advantages are deemed sufficiently important (see, e.g., Kess and Westlin (1982)). It therefore seems more likely that the estate tax motivates closer to 50 percent, and conceivably as much as 75 percent, of lifetime gifts. I will present separate calculations for each of these assumptions (25, 50, and 75 percent).

The actual revenue loss associated with the transfer of an asset worth $1 depends upon several factors. The first is the nature of the tax system prevailing subsequent to the transfer, and the associated marginal tax rates of the concerned parties. I will provide separate calculations for hypothetical policy regimes in which pre-ERTA and ERTA income tax rate schedules are assumed to persist indefinitely, as well as similar calculations for the 1986 TRA. Table 2 contains marginal tax rate assumptions for donors, recipients, and average bondholders for each tax system. Note that I always place the donor in the highest tax bracket. The recipient's marginal tax bracket under the current law corresponds roughly to a married individual reporting taxable income (after deductions) of $30,000 per year. I will return to these assumptions at the end of this section.

The second important factor concerns the propensity of each individual to consume out of current income. I consider two cases. In Case I, the

---

gift and estate taxes, (ii) the reduction in estate tax rates, (iii) the reduced progressivity of income tax rates, and (iv) the liberalization of the unified credit and yearly gift tax exclusion. The first three factors would tend to reduce intra vivos giving, but the fourth has the opposite effect. In view of the enormous importance of the unified credit and yearly exclusion to most individuals, I suspect that the $26.5 billion figure is, if anything, on the low side.

Table 2 MARGINAL INCOME TAX RATE ASSUMPTIONS

	Donor	Recipient	Average bondholder
pre-ERTA	0.7	0.25	0.5
ERTA	0.5	0.25	0.4
TRA of 1986	0.28	0.15	0.23

donor consumes one half of realized nominal income, but the recipient consumes all of it. For Case II, I change the recipient's marginal propensity to consume to 0.7. Both cases reflect an assumption that, over the relevant time period, recipients tend to consume a higher fraction of current income. I expect this pattern because recipients usually anticipate substantial gifts and bequests in the future and are therefore less inclined to save. Although the difference between the marginal propensity to consume of donors and recipients does somewhat affect my results, the actual levels of these parameters appear to make very little difference.

The third factor concerns the timing of the gift. If the donor chose not to make an intra vivos transfer of wealth, the recipient would inherit this wealth upon the donor's death anyway. Consequently, my calculations should reflect lost revenues only between the time of the gift and the donor's eventual death. I will refer to this as the "acceleration factor." In section 3, I argued that good estate planning requires individuals to transfer resources as early in life as possible. Although I present calculations using acceleration factors of five, fifteen, and thirty years, I tend to prefer those based upon the larger figures.

The fourth and final factor concerns the nature of transferred assets. I present separate calculations for stylized stocks and bonds (see the Appendix for details). The characteristics of actual assets might differ from case to case.

Tables 3 through 5 contain results. Each entry in these tables indicates, under specified assumptions, the revenue loss (in cents) induced by a private transfer of assets worth $1. Unfortunately, I have no direct evidence either on actual acceleration factors or on the composition of assets transferred intra vivos. To avoid conveying a false sense of precision, I simply eyeball these tables and select a figure that corresponds roughly to an acceleration factor between fifteen and thirty years and a portfolio consisting of stocks and bonds in equal proportions. For pre-ERTA income tax law, I surmise that the revenue loss per dollar transferred was close to $0.40; for ERTA, it was roughly $0.20; for the 1986 TRA, it is somewhere between $0.10 and $0.20.

In Table 6, I calculate the displacement factor (i.e., the fraction of intra vivos transfers attributable to estate taxation) and the value of lost income tax revenues under alternative sets of assumptions about the revenue loss per dollar of transferred wealth. I take the total value of intra vivos transfers for the target population to be $26.5 billion, which corresponds to the estimated level of such transfers in 1983. My preferred estimates of revenue loss per dollar transferred, combined with a dis-

Table 3   LOSS PER DOLLAR TRANSFERRED—PRE-ERTA (IN CENTS PER DOLLAR)

Acceleration factor	Case I		Case II	
	Bonds	Stocks	Bonds	Stocks
5	16.6	6.4	16.3	6.4
15	45.0	18.3	42.3	18.1
30	77.2	33.8	68.8	31.5

Table 4   LOSS PER DOLLAR TRANSFERRED—ERTA (IN CENTS PER DOLLAR)

Acceleration factor	Case I		Case II	
	Bonds	Stocks	Bonds	Stocks
5	9.4	3.9	9.1	3.8
15	26.7	11.2	24.3	10.9
30	47.0	20.8	40.7	19.5

Table 5   LOSS PER DOLLAR TRANSFERRED—TRA OF 1986 (IN CENTS PER DOLLAR)

Acceleration factor	Case I		Case II	
	Bonds	Stocks	Bonds	Stocks
5	4.9	2.8	4.7	2.7
15	14.1	8.6	12.6	8.3
30	25.5	17.2	21.5	16.0

Table 6   REVENUE LOSS FROM INDUCED INTRA VIVOS TRANSFERS (IN BILLIONS OF DOLLARS)

Revenue loss per dollar of wealth transferred	Displacement factor		
	0.25	0.5	0.75
0.1	0.7	1.3	2.0
0.2	1.3	2.7	4.0
0.3	2.0	4.0	6.0
0.4	2.7	5.3	8.0
0.5	3.3	6.6	10.0

placement factor of 0.5, generate the following conclusions. Under the highly progressive pre-ERTA income tax rates, income tax losses associated with intra vivos transfers induced by the estate tax would amount to between $4.5 billion and $5 billion. Under ERTA rates, this figure would be between $3 billion and $3.5 billion. By making the income tax system less progressive, the 1986 TRA would reduce this loss to perhaps $2 billion (the effect of this Act is somewhat vitiated by the removal of the capital gains exemption). To put these numbers in perspective, one should bear in mind that the federal government collected $5.17 billion from levies on estates with gross values exceeding $300,000 in 1983.[8]

It is unfortunately not entirely appropriate to compare revenue loss calculations based upon the level of intra vivos transfer in 1983 with estate tax revenues in 1983 for two of the three tax regimes. Income tax rates during this period were established by ERTA, and taxpayers probably expected these rates to persist indefinitely. I have already remarked that differentials between marginal personal income tax rates by themselves provide incentives for individuals to make gifts rather than bequests. Had taxpayers expected pre-ERTA income tax rates to prevail after 1983, the division of transfers would probably have been more skewed toward gifts. Accordingly, official estate tax revenues would have been lower, and the true revenue picture would have been even worse. Conversely, had taxpayers expected the 1986 TRA rates to prevail after 1983, the division of transfers might have been more skewed toward bequests. Although this would make the total revenue picture a bit better than my calculations suggest, I suspect that the resulting bias is very small.[9]

At this point, it is appropriate to reflect on the accuracy of the marginal tax rate assumptions employed throughout this exercise. For a number of reasons, these may be erroneous. First, the children of wealthy individuals may in many cases be wealthy themselves, especially after accumulating significant gifts. Second, even comparatively wealthy individuals may have relatively low taxable incomes upon retirement. Third, it is well known that many taxpayers shelter enormous amounts of income. Some may even drive their marginal tax rates to zero through vigorous use of

8. Total estate tax revenues were slightly higher than this, because before 1984 the filing requirement was below $300,000. Unfortunately, the IRS has only released data on estates with gross values exceeding $300,000 for 1983. Accordingly, my calculations are intended to approximate the true net revenue associated with taxing this group.
9. According to my calculations, transferring an asset worth $1 intra vivos lowers the present value of income tax payments by approximately $0.20 under ERTA rates and $0.15 under TRA rates. The effect of this reform on intra vivos transfers should therefore be more or less equal to the effect of cutting the estate tax rate by only 5 percent. Other aspects of the TRA may reduce this effect even further. See the discussion in section 6.3.

provisions such as the investment tax credit. On the other hand, many of the techniques discussed in section 3 for avoiding estate tax also allow such individuals to pass surplus tax shelters to their children, thereby reducing income tax revenues through a related channel. One should also recall that several techniques (i.e., the use of life insurance and pension funds) provide for free accumulation subsequent to the transfer. In addition, children may often use transferred funds to purchase homes, in which case subsequent implicit income escapes taxation entirely. Finally, my calculations completely ignore the revenue losses associated with avoidance activities that reduce gross estates below the filing requirement. It is, however, impossible to account properly for any of these factors without access to currently unavailable IRS records.

5.2 CHARITABLE BEQUESTS

I now turn my attention to charitable bequests. In 1983, decedents with gross estates exceeding $300,000 left approximately $2.5 billion to charities. To calculate the indirect impact on income tax revenues, one must first determine the fraction of this attributable to estate taxation.

I employ Clotfelter's behavioral estimates to compute the impact on charitable bequests of eliminating estate taxation. Using parameters from his most conservative case,[10] I find that charitable bequests would decline by 79.3 percent, or, for 1983, about $2 billion. Such bequests would have all but disappeared for estates under $1 million and would have fallen by more than 76 percent for estates exceeding $1 million.

What is the revenue loss per dollar bequeathed to charity? Here, the relevant comparison is between having the family retain the wealth indefinitely, passing the unconsumed portion from generation to generation, and having it bequeath the same wealth to a tax-exempt institution. I assume that the family is always taxed at the highest statutory marginal rate, and I calculate revenue losses per dollar of transferred assets. Table

10. For estates of less than $1 million, I assume price and income elasticities of -1.6 and 0.4, respectively, and a marginal estate tax rate of 39 percent. For estates exceeding $1 million, these figures are -1.0, 0.4, and 45 percent, respectively.

Table 7   REVENUE LOSS PER DOLLAR OF CHARITABLE BEQUEST (IN CENTS PER DOLLAR)

	Bonds	Stocks
pre-ERTA	142.9	119.8
ERTA	200.0	137.6
TRA OF 1986	68.3	111.6

7 contains results for stylized stocks and bonds under the three tax systems considered earlier. Again I eyeball this table and select figures that roughly reflect a portfolio divided equally between stocks and bonds. Under pre-ERTA income tax law, the revenue loss exceeded $1.50 on each dollar of induced charitable bequests, or (for 1983 levels of charitable bequests) about $3 billion in the aggregate. For rates prevailing subsequent to ERTA, the loss appears to have been about $1.25 on each dollar, or $2.5 billion in the aggregate. Under the tax reform bill, the loss is between $0.80 and $1 on the dollar, or between $1.5 billion and $2 billion in the aggregate.

I have presented estimates of revenue losses from intra vivos giving and charitable bequests for three hypothetical policy regimes in which, respectively, pre-ERTA, ERTA, and TRA income tax rates are assumed to prevail and to persist indefinitely after 1983. Combining these estimates produces striking results. Under my preferred assumptions, estate taxation would have induced a net loss of federal tax revenues roughly equal to $3 billion in 1983 for the highly progressive pre-ERTA income tax regimes. The estate tax probably would have broken even in 1983 or even generated a small loss under the ERTA income tax regime (the total net reduction of income tax revenues, $5.5 billion to $6 billion, slightly exceeds official estate tax revenues for the target group). For rates adopted in the 1986 TRA, indirect losses would have been in the neighborhood of $3.5 billion to $4 billion, or roughly 70 to 80 percent of reported revenues. Even under the more conservative view that estate taxation is responsible for only 25 percent (rather than 50 percent) of intra vivos transfers, true revenues would still have been negative under pre-ERTA income tax rates, perhaps 10 percent of reported revenues under ERTA, and less than half of reported revenues under the TRA rates.

I caution against attaching too much importance to any particular set of numbers. It seems clear that indirect revenue effects may be large relative to reported revenues, but available data simply do not permit precise calculations.

6. Additional Considerations

6.1 ANCILLARY EFFECTS OF SOPHISTICATED ESTATE PLANNING TECHNIQUES

The income tax implications of many estate-planning techniques are complex. In addition to shifting income between taxpayers, some techniques create taxable income, and others generate new shelters. A complete analysis of all indirect effects would represent a major undertaking. For the time being, I simply note that estate planners tend to recommend against techniques in cases where they would create significant income tax liabilities. I have, for instance, already remarked that the preferred stock recapitalization is typically applied only when the parent desires a high level of current income for his or her personal purposes.

6.2 STEP-UP OF BASIS AT DEATH

Another factor that deserves careful consideration is the step-up of basis at death for income tax purposes. If the estate tax causes individuals to transfer assets through gifts that they would otherwise have held until death, then, upon the eventual sale of such assets, total capital gains tax liabilities will be greater. Although this consideration somewhat vitiates our conclusions, I suspect that it is of comparatively minor importance for four reasons.

First, individuals concerned with tax avoidance clearly have an incentive to transfer intra vivos all assets that they do not intend to hold until death before transferring any assets that they never intend to sell. Thus, the relevant question is whether or not donors tend to turn over marginal assets at regular intervals. The evidence presented in section 5 suggests that affluent individuals transfer roughly one third of their total holdings intra vivos and two thirds at death. Thus, as long as these individuals tend to turn over at least one third of their assets, I would not expect them to retain the marginal asset until death.

Second, if a parent is inclined to hold onto an asset for his or her entire life, the heirs may well feel similarly inclined. This is particularly true when the asset in question is a family business or closely held corporation. Thus, the date of eventual sale may be quite distant even at the time of the parent's death, in which case the discounted value of the incremental tax would be quite small.

Third, when individuals hold assets until death, they often go to great lengths to undervalue these assets, thereby minimizing estate tax liability. In fact, Cooper (1979) points out that, through manipulating a series of special factors that cause tax courts to reduce the assessed market value of assets (particularly in closely held corporations), decedents have succeeded in sheltering as much as two thirds of actual asset value for estate tax purposes. Of course, in the process, these decedents also lose the step-up of basis.

Fourth, families that deliberately avoid estate tax may also be fairly sophisticated about avoiding income tax. In particular, by appropriately timing the realization of gains and losses, taxpayers may be able to minimize, or even entirely eliminate, capital gains tax liabilities (see Stiglitz (1983)). Although it appears that very few investors do this in their daily portfolio management (see Poterba (1985)), they may well find it worthwhile to do so when realizing large gains on assets that have been held for a very long time.

Consideration of the step-up of basis at death raises a related issue. This provision probably does not significantly vitiate my conclusions, but it may well deter taxpayers from transferring intra vivos substantially more assets than they do already. Indeed, estate planners agree that by removing the opportunity to pass on property at death free of capital gains tax, Congress would "increase greatly interest in estate tax avoidance" (Cooper (1979, p. 11)). Accordingly, such action would be likely, on balance, to depress federal revenues, contrary to common wisdom.

6.3 THE TAX REFORM ACT OF 1986

Throughout this discussion, I have emphasized that the 1986 TRA reduces the progressivity of federal income tax rates and thereby attenuates the revenue loss per dollar diverted from bequests to gifts. The Act may also have other important effects, to which I have alluded only briefly. Specifically, this decline in progressivity by itself reduces incentives for intra vivos transfers. Under the new Act, we might therefore expect both bequests and estate tax revenues to be higher, whereas the marginal effect on lifetime giving of eliminating the estate tax might well decline.

However, the Act also introduces countervailing forces. First, it eliminates several opportunities for wealthy individuals to accumulate resources tax free (e.g., through individual retirement accounts (IRAs)). Second, it removes numerous tax shelters (e.g., the investment tax credit, the capital gains and dividend exclusions, investment interest deductions, and passive business loss offsets) through which many wealthy individuals currently achieve significant reductions in their marginal tax rates. The net effect of these changes remains to be seen.

In addition, I have been somewhat conservative by assuming that wealthy parents will face marginal income tax rates of 28 percent. The Act includes a surcharge on taxable income between $71,900 and $149,250 for couples ($43,150 and $87,560 for single individuals) that may well produce an effective marginal tax rate of 33 percent for many wealthy taxpayers.

Other provisions also bear on these issues to a lesser degree. Unearned income for children under fourteen is now counted as taxable income for the parent; this somewhat attenuates the ability of parents to arrange significant transfers of resources very early in life. The Act also curtails income splitting through trusts, eliminates the advantages of Clifford and Spousal Remainder Trusts, and strengthens the Generation

Skipping Tax. Yet it is difficult to imagine that these provisions would have a large effect on the overall picture described here.

7. Conclusions

In this paper, I have suggested that the indirect effects of estate levies on personal income tax revenues are extremely large relative to estate tax collections. Although it is very difficult to estimate these effects precisely, in recent years true estate tax revenues may well have been negative. I have emphasized that these conclusions are highly dependent on the progressivity of the personal income tax, but I have also shown that indirect revenue effects would continue to be extremely important even under the new tax reform bill. Accordingly, common planning techniques severely cripple the ability of the federal government to achieve the dual purposes of promoting equity and raising revenue through estate taxation.

Nevertheless, the existence of this tax does appear to effect a diversion of substantial resources (upward of $2 billion per year) to charity, and many may view this as sufficient justification for its retention. Furthermore, avenues for curtailing estate tax and gift tax avoidance have not yet been fully exhausted. By pursuing such avenues, the federal government might well succeed in reducing large concentrations of wealth while significantly enhancing total federal revenue. Yet in the absence of far-reaching reform, it seems unlikely that the estate tax will do much more than benefit charitable causes.

APPENDIX

In this Appendix, we derive formulas that express the value of the government's claim on a privately held asset as a function of the holder's characteristics, the tax system, and the nature of the asset.

First, consider a bond (consol) that pays $\$i$ per year forever. Suppose that the interest rate is i, so the value of the bond is $1. Each year, the bondholder, whose marginal tax rate is m, consumes a fraction γ of nominal after-tax income generated by the bond and reinvests the remainder in new bonds. Bonds pay interest at the beginning of each year starting in year 1, so at the end of year t the investor owns bonds worth

$$(1 + i(1 - m)(1 - \gamma))^t$$

and pays taxes of

$$im(1 + i(1 - m)(1 - \gamma))^{t-1}$$

in period $t + 1$. If $\bar{m}$ is the marginal tax rate of the average bondholder, the present discounted value of this revenue stream through year T is

$$\sum_{t=1}^{T} \frac{im(1 + i(1 - m)(1 - \gamma))^{t-1}}{(1 + (1 - \bar{m})i)^t}$$

$$= m \left[\frac{1}{(1 - \bar{m}) - (1 - \gamma)(1 - m)} \right]$$

$$\left[1 - \left(\frac{1 + i(1 - m)(1 - \gamma)}{1 + (1 - \bar{m})i} \right)^T \right].$$

To calculate the revenue loss associated with transferring the bond from one taxpayer to another for a period of T years, we simply calculate the change in the value of this expression associated with changing the values of m to γ.

Next, consider a stock that, in year 0, represents a claim on capital assets worth \$1. These assets yield after-corporate income tax earnings of \$$\rho$ at the beginning of each year, starting in year 1. The company always pays out the fraction α of earnings as current dividends and retains the remainder, investing it in new capital assets. Thus, at the end of year t, one share of stock represents a claim on capital assets worth $[1 + \rho(1 - \alpha)]^t$.

Let A_τ^t denote the number of shares of vintage τ stock (shares bought in period t) that the investor still holds at the end of period $t \geq \tau$. We take $A_0^0 = 1$. Each year, the investor sells a fraction λ of his stock, irrespective of vintage. Thus,

$$A_\tau^t = A_\tau^\tau (1 - \lambda)^{t-\tau}. \quad (1)$$

He consumes the fraction γ of realized after-tax nominal income and reinvests the proceeds in stock. Once again, we use m to denote the investor's marginal tax rate and $\bar{m}$ to denote the marginal tax rate of the average bondholder. In addition, we assume that the fraction e of realized capital gains is exempt from taxation. Accordingly, in period t, the investor pays taxes of

$$R_t = m \sum_{k=0}^{t-1} A_\tau^t \{\rho\alpha(1 + \rho(1 - \alpha))^{t-1}$$

$$+ \lambda(1 - e)[(1 + \rho(1 - \alpha))^t - (1 + \rho(1 - \alpha))^k]\} \quad (2)$$

and purchases

$$A_t^i = (1 + \rho(1 - \alpha))^{-t} \sum_{k=0}^{t-1} A_k^i \{\rho\alpha(1 - \gamma)(1 - m)(1 + \rho(1 - \alpha))^{t-1}$$
$$+ \lambda(1 + \rho(1 - \alpha))^k [1 + (1 - \gamma)(e + (1 - m)(1 - e))$$
$$((1 + \rho(1 - \alpha))^{t-k} - 1)]\} \quad (3)$$

shares of new stock. Although we were unable to obtain a nice closed-form expression for total revenues, (1)–(3) form a system of difference equations that can be solved numerically. We then value the revenue stream by discounting, as above.

As a final step, we relate ρ to i through capital market equilibrium conditions. Under traditional views of capital market equilibrium (see Poterba and Summers (1985)),

$$\rho = \frac{i(1 - m)}{\alpha(1 - m) + (1 - \alpha)(1 - z)},$$

where

$$z = \frac{\lambda(1 - e)m}{\lambda + i(1 - m)}$$

is the effective tax rate on capital gains (see King and Fullerton (1984)).

REFERENCES

Barthold, Thomas, and Robert Plotnick. 1984. Estate taxation and other determinants of charitable bequests. *National Tax Journal* 37: 255–37.

Bentz, Mary. 1985. Estate tax returns, 1983. *SOI Bulletin* 4:1–12.

Boskin, Michael. 1976. Estate taxation and charitable bequests. *Journal of Public Economics* 5:27–56.

Brosterman, Robert. 1977. *The complete estate planning guide.* New York: McGraw-Hill.

Clay, William. 1982. *The Dow Jones-Irwin guide to estate planning.* Homewood, Ill.: Dow Jones-Irwin.

Clotfelter, Charles. 1985. *Federal tax policy and charitable giving.* Chicago: University of Chicago Press.

Esperti, Robert, and Renno Peterson. 1983. *The handbook of estate planning.* New York: McGraw-Hill.

Feldstein, Martin. 1974. Financing the evaluation of public expenditure. In *Public finance and stabilization policy,* eds. W. Smith and J. Culbertson. Amsterdam: North-Holland.

———. 1977. Charitable bequests, estate taxation, and intergenerational wealth transfers. In *Research papers*, 1485–1500. Commission on Private Philanthropy and Public Needs 3. Washington, D.C.: Treasury Department.

Kess, Sidney, and Bertil Westlin. 1982. *CCH estate planning guide*. Chicago: Commerce Clearing House.

King, Mervyn. 1977. *Public policy and the corporation*. London: Chapman and Hall.

King, Mervyn, and Don Fullerton. 1984. *The taxation of income from capital*. Chicago: University of Chicago Press.

Kotlikoff, Lawrence, and Lawrence Summers. 1981. The role of intergenerational transfers in aggregate capital accumulation. *Journal of Political Economy* 84: 706–32.

McNess, Stephen. 1973. Deductibility of charitable bequests. *National Tax Journal* 26:81–98.

Milam, Edward, and D. Larry Crumbley. 1977. *Estate planning—After the 1976 Tax Reform Act*. New York: McGraw-Hill.

Poterba, James. 1985. How burdensome are capital gains taxes. MIT. Mimeo.

Poterba, James, and Lawrence Summers. 1985. The economic effects of dividend taxation. In *Recent advances in corporate finance*, eds. Edward I. Altman and Marti G. Subrahmanyam, 227–84. Homewood, Ill.: Richard Irwin.

Stiglitz, Joseph. 1983. Some aspect of the taxation of capital gains. *Journal of Public Economics* 21:257–94.

U.S. Internal Revenue Service. 1979. *Statistics of income, 1976 estate tax*. Washington, D.C.: U.S. Government Printing Office.

Michael J. Boskin and Douglas J. Puffert
Standard University and NBER, Stanford University

Social Security and the American Family

Expected Social Security retirement benefits are the largest single "asset" available to most Americans. Social Security is also the source of the largest tax burden for a majority of American workers. Because the program is so large and complex, it is important to understand the investment deal it offers persons and families in different situations, as well as the aggregate financial and economic implications of the program and any change in it. Expected benefits depend on a variety of factors, such as one's marital status, age, sex, age-earnings profile, length of career, number of children, other income sources in retirement, and so on.

The purpose of this paper is to discuss a number of important issues associated with the "deal" and incentives projected to be offered by the current Social Security system, especially with respect to its treatment of the family. By treatment of the family, we mean the expected benefits, taxes, rates of return, and marginal benefits per incremental dollar of taxes paid for persons in different family situations: married versus single, number of earners in the family and the division of earnings between them, the special situation of widows and divorcees, and so on.

Although a number of authors have commented on various features of the Social Security system affecting people in these different situations,[1]

We wish to thank Larry Summers for useful suggestions and the Stanford University Center for Economic Policy Research and the NBER for support of this research. The research supported here is part of the NBER's Research Program in Taxation and Project in Government Budgets. Any opinions expressed are those of the authors and not those of the NBER. Some of the material in this paper elaborates work presented in M. Boskin, L. Kotlikoff, D. Puffert, and J. Shoven, Social Security: A financial appraisal across and within generations, NBER Working Paper no. 1891, April 1986.
1. See, for example, essays in Burkhauser and Holden (1982) and the discussion in Boskin et al. (1986).

we believe it is worthwhile to refocus attention on these specific issues in light of some important factors. Among these are the substantial changes introduced by the 1983 Social Security amendments, the changing actuarial projections used as the intermediate assumptions in the last few years, the dramatic changes in life expectancies, and the rapid change of the structure of American families toward more episodes of divorce, more single person households, and more common and lengthier widowhood than several decades ago, to name a few.

We begin by pointing out that Social Security offers very different ex ante "deals" and marginal returns for incremental taxes paid to persons of different income, family status, age, sex, and income. Although this may or may not be desirable, the extent of the differences is not widely appreciated. In particular, a substantial fraction of some subgroups in the population receive virtually nothing back for incremental taxes paid. Therefore, an important problem of Social Security is that it may rightly be perceived primarily as a tax and not as a savings scheme.

Among the features that treat persons of different family status differently in Social Security are the following:

1. The progressivity of the benefit formula
2. Survivors' benefits
3. Spousal benefits
4. Rules governing eligibility of divorced persons
5. The ceiling on Social Security taxable earnings
6. The taxation of one half of benefits over a certain income level for persons receiving benefits
7. Child survivors' benefits
8. The person's age cohort reflecting the maturity of the system and, therefore, their entire tax history.

Each of these factors interacts with the important non–Social Security features of differential life expectancies for different groups, most importantly for the issues discussed here, for maless and females, and the differential wage-level trajectories typical of males and females in the labor force.

There is a substantial variation in the typical Social Security benefits of female new beneficiaries, depending upon whether they receive the spouse benefit, their own worker benefit, or, in the case of widows, survivor benefits. Of new female beneficiaries in 1982, 64 percent were part of married couples, and 24 percent were widows. For the former, the most common benefit was the spouse benefit; for the latter, the survivor benefit. Only about 30 percent of women who were ever married received benefits based on their own earnings history.[2]

As can be seen from this list of features of Social Security and other factors affecting the deal and the marginal linkages of benefits and taxes, the situation is rather complex. To clarify these issues, we organize the paper as follows. Section 1 presents a cursory literature review and a description of our data and methodology. Section 2 presents some comparisons among households with different earnings splits and different levels of earnings. We examine a single-earner couple and examples of two-earner couples where the earnings split is two thirds and one third between the husband and wife or fifty-fifty between the husband and wife. We present the expected present value of taxes paid, benefits received, and transfers, and, therefore, the expected internal rate of return on taxes paid for three total family earnings levels indexed to 1985: $10,000, $30,000, and $50,000. These projections are made for the cohort of persons born in 1945.[3] Our primary purpose here is not to discuss the intergenerational issues but rather the intragenerational issues of differential treatment of persons in different family status. The differences often amount to more than the value of a typical family house.

Also presented in section 2 is a discussion of the second-earners' range of zero-marginal return. The issue here is how much a wife must earn, for a given level of her husband's earnings, before she begins to receive any incremental return for the Social Security taxes she pays. We also discuss single males versus single females, and singles versus couples. The presence of spousal and survivors' benefits clearly changes the deal offered to couples versus singles.

Section 3 analyzes the marriage penalty or subsidy, that is, how a man and a woman fare under Social Security if they marry relative to how they fare if they stay single. The amounts involved are substantial, exceeding the more hotly debated marriage penalty in the personal income tax.

Section 4 discusses the situation for widows and divorcees. We present similar information on the present value of benefits, taxes, transfers, and rates of return, including those in which the widow worked or did not work prior to the assumed date of death of the husband. We also present the various situations defining the range of earnings widows would make without receiving any incremental Social Security benefits, or for nonworking wives, who start work at two thirds of their hus-

2. Social Security Administration (1985).
3. Boskin, et al. (1986) presents details for other cohorts.

bands' wage upon widowhood, the age after which they would receive no incremental Social Security benefits despite payment of substantial taxes. Analogous results are presented for divorcees. For the latter, a tremendous incentive exists to postpone divorce until after ten years of marriage. The financial stake can exceed $50,000.

Section 5 discusses the issue of the marginal linkage of benefits and taxes in more detail. The relation of the expected present value of benefits received for an incremental dollar of taxes paid varies substantially by family status and earnings level.

Section 6 discusses some parallel stories for the cohort born in 1975, given the actuarial projections of the Social Security Administration, ignoring any potential long-term financial solvency problems of the system, and accounting for several changes relative to the 1945 cohort.

Section 7 offers a brief conclusion and summary of the results.

1. The Present Study in Perspective

Several studies have attempted to estimate the "deal" different households receive or can expect to receive in the future from the Social Security retirement program. It is well known that the early cohorts of retirees had very large rates of return on their taxes and that future retirees, especially wealthy ones, will not fare well relative to rates of return available on private assets.[4]

The primary contribution of this study is to update the results to the post-1983 amendments situation (of the studies cited, only Pellechio and Goodfellow (1983), Boskin (1986), and Boskin et al. (1986) do so), allow for recent changes in the Social Security Administration's actuarial assumptions about future economic and demographic factors, present a wider range of cases, examine the marginal linkage between taxes paid and benefits received, and focus in particular on the situation of women in these updated cases (supplementing the important work in the Burkhauser and Holden volume).

We use a computer simulation to convert assumptions about households' wages, expected mortality, and economywide growth in real wages into expected present values of Social Security taxes, benefits, net transfers, and internal rates of return. We also thus derive the mar-

4. A sample of such studies includes Boskin, Avrin, and Cone (1983), Hurd and Shoven (1985), Boskin (1986), Pellechio and Goodfellow (1983), Flowers (1977), Ricardo-Campbell (1977), and several studies in the book by Burkhauser and Holden (1982), of particular importance because it focuses on the role of women in the Social Security system as it existed at the time the essays were written and under various alternatives. See also Boskin et al. (1986) and the survey by Thompson (1983).

ginal linkage between incremental taxes paid and incremental benefits received.[5]

2. Comparisons Among Households (1945 Cohort)

Social Security—both when it was introduced and every time it was expanded—has been a major vehicle for transferring resources from the younger, richer, working generation to the older, poorer, retired generation. But these transfers do not occur uniformly across different types of families. Tables 1 and 3 show how the expected present value of benefits, taxes, and transfers for single men and women of different income levels and for married couples vary with different levels and composition of income. In Table 1, we note that moving from single-earner households to an identical earnings stream split between the couple reduces the expected present value of benefits and the expected present value of transfers substantially for all three earnings levels considered. The "deal" as measured by the internal rate of return on expected taxes paid worsens as we move toward a more equal division of the earnings and, obviously, as we move for any type of household to higher earnings levels. For example, a couple with $30,000 (at the 1985 wage index) in which the husband was the sole earner would receive a 2.3 percent internal rate of return on $136,498 taxes paid and therefore suffer a $27,370 loss, discounting benefits and taxes at a 3 percent real rate of return. The corresponding numbers for a two third–one third and one half–one half split

---

5. Obviously, to conduct these analyses, one must make various assumptions. We consider households that vary in several attributes: marital status, year of birth, the amount of total earnings and its division between wife and husband. We calculate expected taxes and benefits using mortality probabilities computed separately for males and females, and separate mortality tables are used for different cohorts. The tables used are those prepared for the intermediate assumptions in the 1983 *Report of the Trustees of the Old Age and Survivors and Disability Insurance Trust Funds*.

All earnings levels reported in tables below correspond directly to twenty-five-year olds in 1985. We assume that wages for males increase 1 percent per year of age, and for females 0.5 percent per year of age, until age fifty. Thus, for the 1945 cohort, male wages in 1985 will be about 16 percent higher than earnings levels listed, since the males will be forty rather than twenty-five, and female wages will be nearly 8 percent higher for the same reason. Earnings levels also vary annually with economywide wage growth. We use the Social Security Administration's intermediate wage growth assumption (roughly 1.5 percent per year beyond inflation) from the 1985 *Report of the Trustees of the Old Age and Survivors and Disability Insurance Trust Funds*.

We estimate the expected taxation of one half of future benefits to the extent that that portion of one's benefits plus other adjusted gross income exceeds the nonindexed threshold levels of $25,000 for singles and $32,000 for couples. We use the tax law in existence when this paper was written. The results would vary somewhat given the reduction in marginal tax rates in the tax law about to be phased in.

For further details, see Boskin et al. (1986).

of income, adding to $30,000, are 1.75 percent and 1.45 percent for the rate of return and transfers of −$48,715 and −$54,199. Thus, for the same earnings levels, we see the pattern repeated. Not only does the rate of return vary by family type and earnings level, but there is a substantial interaction between the two. For example, for single-earner households, the rate of return received by a $50,000 earning household is about one half that for the $10,000 household (1.95 percent versus 3.74 percent), whereas for the households with the equal division of earnings the comparable numbers are 0.61 percent versus 3.81 percent, a fivefold rather than a twofold ratio. Clearly, the interaction of the spouse benefit and the incremental taxes paid as the spouse earns a greater amount of taxable income worsens the deal substantially.

Table 2 reports the range of zero-incremental returns for the 1945 cohort for the second earner. For the same three earnings levels for the primary earner, we derive the mininum earnings level per year to receive any incremental return from Social Security taxes paid by the second earner (rather than just collecting the spouse's benefits and "losing" all Social Security taxes paid). Note that this calculation understates the minimum earnings level necessary for second earners with intermittent

Table 1   COMPARISON ACROSS DIVISIONS OF HOUSEHOLD EARNINGS FOR 1945 COHORT, VARIOUS EARNINGS LEVELS (1985 DOLLARS DISCOUNTED AT RATE 3 PERCENT TO 1985)

Division of earnings (Husband-wife)	Total family earnings level (At 1985 wage index)		
	10,000	30,000	50,000
1–0 (single earner)			
P.V. benefits	62,679	109,128	100,503
P.V. taxes	48,951	136,498	140,253
P.V. transfer	13,727	−27,370	−39,750
Rate of return	3.74%	2.30%	1.95%
⅔–⅓			
P.V. benefits	53,293	96,044	108,428
P.V. taxes	48,264	144,760	218,119
P.V. transfer	5,029	−48,715	−109,689
Rate of return	3.30%	1.75%	0.80%
½–½			
P.V. benefits	50,936	89,578	109,457
P.V. taxes	47,926	143,777	233,433
P.V. transfer	3,010	−54,199	−123,975
Rate of return	3.18%	1.54%	0.61%

work histories because it is assumed that this 1985 earnings level will continue each year until retirement.[6] For those who step out of the work force for a long time, the numbers would be much larger. As an example, consider the primary earner who is earning $30,000 per year. If the spouse goes to work, he or she would have to earn almost $10,000 per year before receiving *any* incremental return. In short, the first $9,600 per year of earnings upon which over $1,000 of taxes would be paid (by the employee and employer) would result in no incremental return to the Social Security benefits for the couple. This is another way to view the differences between the different earnings splits of families.

In short, there is a substantial tax on married women's labor force participation through the spouse's benefit. Until the married woman's own earnings history (if any) is sufficient to produce benefits beyond the spouse's benefit, the entire Social Security payroll tax is a pure tax, with no corresponding presumption of future incremental Social Security benefits. Since the Social Security payroll tax for Old Age and Survivors Insurance exceeds 10 percent and is expected to rise, this is a substantial extra tax bite at the margin (we make the usual presumption that the employee bears both the employer and the employee component of the tax to be a reasonable first approximation). Under the new income tax reforms, this raises marginal tax rates about 70 percent and 35 percent for those in the 15 percent and 28 percent brackets, respectively.

Table 3 presents a comparison among single-earner couples, single males, and single females at various earnings levels. The story is much the same as that reported above for single-earner versus two-earner couples, although singles, especially single males, fare especially poorly. The reason why single-earner couples do so well reflects the extra benefits due to the joint survivor nature of Social Security benefits for the same taxes paid. Different life expectancies are responsible for the male and female differences among singles. The single-earner couple collects the spouse

6. The retirement benefit of the spouse is based on an average indexed monthly earning that would include a substantial number of years of coverage.

Table 2   SECOND EARNER'S RANGE OF ZERO INCREMENTAL RETURN (1945 COHORT)

First earner's earning level	10,000	30,000	50,000
Second earner's minimum earnings level to receive an incremental return[a]	2,900	9,600	10,000

[a]In this simulation, both earners' wages increase at the male age profile of wages.

benefit while both are alive, and survivor benefits are received by a surviving spouse if the single earner has died first. Clearly, in the case of singles, there are by definition no survivors to receive such benefits. Hence, the expected present value of taxes paid is quite similar at each earnings level for each of the three types of households, but the expected present value of benefits differs enormously.

For example, at the $30,000 level the expected present value of taxes is about $136,000 for single males and single-earner couples, and only a few thousand dollars less for single females.[7] However, the expected present value of benefits ranges from $52,000 for single males to $109,000 for the single-earner couple.

In brief summary, these tables reveal enormous differences in the expected present value of benefits and rates of return on taxes paid to different family types at each earnings level and the important interaction of family type and earnings level in determining the "deal" various families get from Social Security. Although these data are interesting and instructive, we need to probe more deeply into the situation facing wid-

7. The difference is due to assumptions concerning mortality probabilities and how earnings rise with age.

Table 3   COMPARISON AMONG SINGLE-EARNER COUPLES, SINGLE MALES, AND SINGLE FEMALES OF 1945 COHORT, VARIOUS EARNINGS LEVELS (1985 DOLLARS DISCOUNTED AT RATE 3 PERCENT TO 1985)

Family type	Earnings level (At 1985 wage index)		
	10,000	30,000	50,000
Single-Earner Couple			
P.V. benefits	62,679	109,128	100,503
P.V. taxes	48,951	136,498	140,253
P.V. transfer	13,727	−27,370	−39,750
Rate of return	3.74%	2.30%	1.95%
Single Male			
P.V. benefits	29,913	52,282	48,532
P.V. taxes	48,951	136,498	140,253
P.V. transfer	−19,038	−84,216	−91,721
Rate of return	1.42%	−0.25%	−0.60%
Single Family			
P.V. benefits	40,306	71,715	69,590
P.V. taxes	46,901	130,802	144,723
P.V. transfer	−6,595	−59,087	−75,133
Rate of return	2.55%	1.13%	0.68%

owed and divorced persons. This is especially true because of the likelihood that they will be receiving benefits that are quite low, that they may well be the group in the population most likely to be poor in old age,[8] and because changing family conditions and life expectancies in the United States render the treatment of widows and divorced persons increasingly important in the evaluation of the adequacy and cost effectiveness of Social Security benefits.

3. Marriage and Children

Social Security creates important incentives and provides various subsidies or penalties to family creation and dissolution. For example, there is a huge financial stake in staying married for ten years for those contemplating divorce after a few years of marriage (detailed more fully in section 4). Likewise, Social Security provides some auxiliary benefits for children, especially child survivor benefits. But because of the evolution of the system, these same children will in the future likely pay much more in taxes than they will receive in benefits. Finally, because Social Security provides both spouse benefits and spousal survivor benefits, and also because marriage may raise the marginal income tax rate that is applied to one's benefits, a single male and a single female contemplating marriage may face a marriage penalty or subsidy.

Table 4 presents calculations of this marriage subsidy or penalty for various combinations of the (newly married) husband's and wife's earnings levels, assuming that both spouses continue working on the same earnings path. One very important Social Security subsidy is demonstrated in the entries in the table with zero for "wife's earnings" and in the columns for "wife stops working." In each of these situations, the couple gets a subsidy given by the spouse's benefit. The subsidy exceeds $50,000 in virtually every case. Thus, these couples do much better under Social Security married than as singles. Although the wife leaving her job upon marriage is an extreme case, we present these numbers to indicate the value of that "option" to the married couple over its lifetime. For those couples where both spouses continue to work *and* the wife's earnings are sufficient to generate her own worker's benefits, the table also demonstrates that higher income taxes paid on a portion of Social Security benefits more than offsets the extra value of the survivor's benefit based on the husband's (possibly high) earnings. This penalty can amount to $9,000 or $10,000 when discounted at 3 percent, considerably more

8. See Boskin and Shoven (1986).

when discounted at lower rates. This sum is modest relative to the subsidies to the nonworking spouses.

That is not the end of the story, however. Most of those singles who marry will have children, and they in turn will probably pay considerably more in taxes than they receive back in benefits. Although this is unlikely to be of major concern in marriage or fertility decisions, it is interesting to note the expected change in family finances, including the impact from the children's taxes and benefits. Such hypothetical scenarios are presented in Table 5. For several combinations of parents' earnings and children's expected earnings, we see that the "bad deal" the children get offsets the subsidy to nonworking spouses and substantially increases the marriage penalty for working spouses. The table considers hypothetical singles from the 1945 cohort who marry and (for simplicity) have two children (one male, one female) in 1975. We assume that the

Table 4   MARRIAGE SUBSIDY OR PENALTY (1945 COHORT; 1985 DOLLARS DISCOUNTED AT 3 PERCENT TO 1985)

Husband's earnings level	Wife's earnings level	Wife keeps working (Change in benefits = change in net transfer)	Wife stops working		
			Change in benefits	Change in taxes	Change in transfer
$40,000	$40,000	−8,749	−25,814	−117,089	91,275
	20,000	−4,471	−14,568	−69,496	54,928
	0	54,388	—	—	—
$30,000	$30,000	−9,551	−25,305	−103,170	77,865
	15,000	3,214	−2,051	−52,122	50,071
	0	56,846	—	—	—
$20,000	$20,000	−4,656	−18,672	−69,514	50,842
	10,000	9,422	6,584	−34,748	41,332
	0	47,050	—	—	—

Table 5   "DEAL" FOR FAMILY (INCLUDING ESTIMATED TREATMENT OF CHILDREN) FROM MARRIAGE AND CHILDREN[a] (1945 AND 1975 COHORTS; 1985 DOLLARS, DISCOUNTED AT 3 PERCENT TO 1985)

Husband's earnings level	Wife's earnings level	Wife works	Wife stops working
$30,000	$30,000	−41,907	45,509
	15,000	−29,142	17,715
	0	24,490	—

[a] Ignores value of child survivor benefits.

children have one earner with the same relative earnings as their father.[9] Since each future couple has two sets of parents, we attribute one half of the deal to each child in this couple.

Social Security provides various incentives and redistributions because of its many rules and features, such as the spouse benefit, the survivor benefit, and taxation of earnings of individuals (as opposed to families). In some cases, as documented above, the redistribution is large relative to the disputes over features of the personal income tax. Some of the marriage subsidies are much larger than the annual small marriage penalty in the income tax. The marriage penalties, combined with the poor deal for children can be many times the marriage penalty in the income tax. Whether the marginal incentives are sufficient to change behavior in labor force participation and family formation and dissolution is less obvious. Clearly, some of the incentives, such as staying married a tenth year if contemplating divorce after nine years of marriage, are likely to be so strong as to affect behavior noticeably. That the spouse benefit renders the payroll tax a pure tax with no incremental return undoubtedly reduces the labor supply of married women. Other incentives exist, but they may only affect behavior slightly, if at all.

4. Widowhood and Divorce

Tables 6 and 7 present comparable information to that presented above for archetypical situations for widowed and divorced women. Comparable information could be generated for widowers and divorced men, but they are, at least historically, of somewhat less interest given the much higher male labor force participation rates than those for females. The projected treatment of widows born in 1945 at various earnings levels and discounted to constant 1985 dollars reveals some interesting facts. Our archetypical situation contemplates a widow who loses her husband when they are both age fifty. The expected present value of benefits includes, where applicable, survivor benefits and retired worker benefits. The present value of taxes includes taxes paid by the husband before his death. As we can see by comparing Tables 6 and 1, widows who lose their husbands at relatively early ages get a much poorer internal rate of return than surviving couples of comparable earnings levels.

The rates of return for widows in the middle and upper earnings range are quite low, even negative for those who were working and will continue to work after their husbands' death. Take the example of the one half–one half earnings split: the widow who is from a couple where each

9. Note that this means the negative transfers are the smallest for any of the family patterns.

Table 6   TREATMENT OF WIDOWS[a] OF 1945 COHORT, VARIOUS
EARNINGS LEVELS (1985 DOLLARS DISCOUNTED AT RATE 3 PERCENT
TO 1985)

Division of earnings (Husband-wife)	Total family earnings level (At 1985 wage index)		
	10,000	30,000	50,000
1–0 (single earner)			
P.V. benefits	41,025	74,012	69,201
P.V. taxes[b]	36,056	97,771	101,570
P.V. transfer	4,969	−23,759	−32,369
Rate of return	3.33%	2.28%	2.00%
⅔–⅓			
P.V. benefits	33,704	57,930	69,115
P.V. taxes[b]	40,141	120,390	181,795
P.V. transfer	−6,437	−62,460	−112,680
Rate of return	2.53%	1.01%	0.30%
½–½			
P.V. benefits	34,068	58,954	73,405
P.V. taxes[b]	42,189	126,566	204,742
P.V. transfer	−8,121	−67,612	−131,337
Rate of return	2.40%	0.85%	0.07%

[a]That is, widows who lose their husbands at age fifty.

[b]Includes taxes paid by husband before his death.

Table 7   WIDOWS' AND DIVORCED WOMEN'S RANGE OF ZERO
INCREMENTAL BENEFITS (1945 COHORT)

Husband's Earnings Level	10,000	30,000	50,000
Widow's minimum earnings level to receive an incremental return[a]	7,500	21,000	22,000
Latest age at which widowhood occurs, and widow first begins work at ⅔ of husband's wage, to receive an incremental return[a]	39	41	45
Divorced woman's minimum earnings level to receive an incremental return[a]	2,900	9,600	10,000
Latest age at which divorce occurs, and divorced woman first begins work at ⅔ of husband's wage, to receive an incremental return[a]	51	49	54

[a]In this simulation, both earners' wages increase at the male age profile of wages.

earner earned $25,000 (adjusted to the 1985 wage level) would lose $131,000 because she and her deceased husband paid in taxes of $204,000 and received back $73,000 in expected present value of benefits. The internal rate of return is barely over zero percent. Only for single-earner, low-income households do widows receive a rate of return comparable to our assumed 3 percent discount rate.

In comparing similar columns and rows from Table 6 with those in Table 1, note several important facts. First, Table 1 is completely ex ante; that is, everything is in expected value terms.[10] Table 6 is somewhat ex post: we have presumed that the husband survived to age fifty and the widow to retirement age, and we use mortality probabilities of 1 at age fifty for the husband and the life table mortality probabilities beyond age sixty-six for the surviving wife. Second, we assume that widows of single-earner households do not go back to work. Such a widow may in fact begin work but will not be able to work enough to increase her benefits beyond the spousal survivor benefit. Because she will pay substantial taxes with no return in benefit, she will be worse off than the table actually suggests. The same is true for the two thirds–one third earnings split; continuing to work at the same earnings level, the widow will get more as a survivor than as a retired worker, and hence get nothing for incremental taxes paid for the remainder of her work life. However, when each spouse earns half the income, the widow will get more as a retired worker than as a survivor if she continues to work at the same earnings level. Third, we ignore the possibility of remarriage for the purpose of this calculation.

Again, as for married women, we present the range of conditions generating zero incremental benefits for widows and divorced women. These conditions are presented for three presumed (1985 indexed) husbands' earnings levels: $10,000, $30,000, and $50,000. The data are presented in two ways. First, we consider the minimum earnings level necessary for a woman to receive an incremental return. Second, we consider the latest age at which widowhood or divorce could occur in order for a woman to receive an incremental benefit if the woman only then first begins work at two thirds of the husband's wage rate (slightly higher than the average ratio of female to male wages). Thus, in the first panel we note that for a husband's earning level of $10,000, a woman who is widowed at age fifty would need to earn $7,500 (indexed) per year for the remainder of her work life to receive any incremental return whatsoever. All taxes paid under $7,500 (indexed) would result in zero incremental return. The analogous numbers for widows of husbands earning $30,000 a year and

10. Thus Table 1 includes the case of early widowhood weighted by its probability.

$50,000 a year are indeed large: $21,000 and $22,000, respectively. Thus, a widow who returns to work full time for the remainder of her work life, earns up to $20,000, and is responsible for joint employee and employer payroll taxes for retirement of well over $2,000 a year would be receiving no incremental return.

In the second panel, we present the latest age at which widowhood could occur, and the widow begin work, for the widow to receive an incremental return. For the three earnings levels, these ages are 39, 41, and 45. Thus, only a woman widowed quite young who goes back to work earning two thirds of her husband's wages over her remaining work life will receive any incremental return. The rate of return will still be quite modest, because the contributions by and on behalf of her husband will generate no return for she will switch from survivor benefits to retired worker benefits.

The table also presents analogous information for divorced women. Recall that women who are married for less than ten years do not "vest" in the husband's earnings records. Conversely, any given earnings history may generate more than one divorced person's benefit if there were two or more marriages that lasted ten years or more, apparently a growing phenomenon in the United States. Women do not lose from remarriage because they can get benefits based on a former spouse's earnings history. The corresponding earnings levels for women married for more than ten years, and hence entitled to the spouse benefit based on their ex-husband's entire earnings history, to receive any incremental benefits at all are $2,900, $9,600, and $10,000, considerably less than for widows.[11]

Correspondingly, the latest age at which divorce could occur (assuming on remarriage) and the divorced worker go to work at two thirds of the husband's earnings rate and receive *any* incremental benefits are 51, 49, and 54, respectively. If the woman's earnings record is considerably smaller than two thirds of the projected earnings of the divorced husband, these ages would be considerably younger. Of course, a divorced person who is not vested in her spouse's earnings history receives incremental benefits as soon as she goes to work.

These data reveal several interesting facts. First, there is an enormous incentive to postpone divorce until the ten-year "vesting" period is completed. For example, in a one-earner couple with the husband earning $30,000 indexed to 1985, a divorce after nine years of marriage would cost the divorcee about $35,000–$40,000 discounted to 1985! This is more than the median net financial assets of U.S. households.

11. They need only achieve a retired worker benefit equal to one half that of their husbands to switch from a spouse benefit to their own retirement benefit.

In an era when life expectancies are growing (especially for women who have already reached traditional retirement ages) and when divorce and remarriage have become much more prevalent, these enormous variations in the treatment of different individuals, some of whom may differ little in when their widowhood or divorce occurred, suggest that continued pressure will be placed upon Social Security to reform the nature of its taxation and benefit payments to families and individuals.

5. The Marginal Linkage Between Benefits and Taxes

We have presented several types of information for various types of households, including widows and divorcees, traditional one-earner and two-earner couples, single males, and single females. Most of the information concerns the expected present value of total taxes paid, expected present value of total benefits received, and, therefore, the lifetime transfer, as well as the internal rate of return, on expected taxes paid. We have discussed some issues of incremental linkage, such as the age or the earnings at which a person would start to earn their retired worker benefits and begin to receive an incremental return on their taxes, switching over from spousal, survivor, or divorced person's retirement benefit.

It is instructive to note the discounted expected *marginal* benefit for marginal taxes paid (we assume the extra taxes are spread over the lifetime in proportion to earnings). We present this information in Table 8 to give some idea of the marginal linkage for archetypical couples and singles. For each of our archetypical earnings levels, the table considers for male or female the discounted expected extra benefits paid for a dollar of extra taxes spread over the lifetime. These data are for the cohort born in 1960, who have recently entered the labor force, and are discounted to 1985 with a 3 percent real discount rate. Four cases of family status are presented: one-earner couple, two-earner couple where each is presumed to earn one half of the earnings, single males, and single females. Some remarkable facts emerge.

In *no* case is the marginal linkage as high as one hundred percent. Nobody gets back an incremental dollar for an incremental dollar of tax paid. The figures presented in Table 8 range from a marginal linkage as low as $0.12 on the dollar for a female in a high-wage, two-earner couple and $0.15 on the dollar for a single male of middle income to $0.73 on the dollar for a low-income male in a one-earner couple. Note that for some of the entries in the table the particular case involved is at the maximum tax; hence, there can be no additional taxes considered as part of this experiment. Note also that in a one-earner couple, the female receives nothing for an incremental dollar of taxes paid. The female would have to earn a substantial amount of earnings to generate expected Social Security benefits in excess of the spouse's benefit received by the couple independent of any earnings she may produce.

For two-earner couples, the discounted expected incremental benefit per incremental tax paid differs for males and females. The extra linkage to male taxes for a couple involves the joint survivor annuity nature of Social Security benefits in the single-earner case and the survivor benefits for the wife in the two-earner case. The reduced linkage for two-earner wives occurs because she collects survivor benefits rather than retired worker benefits after her husband dies.

There are many reasons why we might be interested in marginal linkage in addition to or instead of total returns. First, to the extent that the complicated system eventually becomes understood,[12] it is the marginal linkage that determines the extent to which Social Security's payroll tax will be thought of as a tax rather than as forced saving. To the extent that it is thought of as a tax, it will substantially increase the effective marginal tax rate on labor earnings, worsening the labor market distortion caused by higher marginal tax rates. Finally, equity may be thought of as equal treatment of people at the margin as well as on average. We make no claim for this, but identical treatment of people at the margin can lead to vastly different treatment of people on average, and vice versa. We merely present the numbers for additional information.

12. This may be more reflective of a person getting close to retirement, attempting to gather information and to calculate what their benefits will be under different stages of retirement and continued earnings levels than for the general population.

Table 8   DISCOUNTED EXPECTED MARGINAL BENEFIT PER MARGINAL TAXES PAID, WITH EXTRA TAXES SPREAD OVER LIFETIME (FOR 1960 COHORT AT 3 PERCENT REAL DISCOUNT RATE)

Earnings level	Contributor	1-Earner couple	2-Earner couple	Single male	Single female
$10,000	Male	.730	.546	.348	—
	Female	0	.301	—	.474
$30,000	Male	.338	.517	.150	—
	Female	0	.286	—	.205
$50,000	Male	*	.216	*	—
	Female	0	.119	—	*

*At maximum tax.

6. Evolution of the System

Tables 9, 10, and 11 present some information, comparable to that presented earlier, for a later cohort, that born in 1975. Obviously, projecting the future over the lifetimes of these individuals and families is subject to a greater range of error than for the younger cohorts. Among the reasons are the potential financial solvency problems that Social Security may face in the future, which include the expected long-term actuarial deficit in Old Age, Survivors, and Disability Insurance (OASDI), which may become larger due to the reduced reflow of income credited to Social Security when the new tax bill passes (which will lower marginal tax rates and hence the tax rate applicable to one half of Social Security benefits received by well-off retirees); and, indeed, Social Security's retirement and disability funds are scheduled to accrue immense surpluses from around 1990 to 2020, which are needed if we are to avoid drastic tax increases when the baby-boom generation retires. Of course, we have no guarantee that we will be able to accrue such massive surpluses. (Boskin (1986) estimates that they will accumulate to a size approximately that of the entire present national debt.) There may be political pressure to use

Table 9   COMPARISON ACROSS DIVISIONS OF HOUSEHOLD EARNINGS FOR 1975 COHORT, VARIOUS EARNINGS LEVELS (1985 DOLLARS DISCOUNTED AT RATE 3 PERCENT TO 1985)

Division of earnings (Husband-wife)	Total family earnings level (At 1985 wage index)		
	10,000	30,000	50,000
1–0 (single earner)			
P.V. benefits	37,775	67,464	63,052
P.V. taxes	33,273	99,820	112,081
P.V. transfer	4,502	−32,356	−49,029
Rate of return	3.37%	1.85%	1.36%
⅔–⅓			
P.V. benefits	32,052	58,835	67,321
P.V. taxes	32,796	98,387	159,560
P.V. transfer	−744	−39,552	−92,239
Rate of return	2.93%	1.49%	0.45%
½–½			
P.V. benefits	30,587	54,874	67,152
P.V. taxes	32,560	97,680	162,800
P.V. transfer	−1,973	−42,806	−95,648
Rate of return	2.82%	1.29%	0.34%

Table 10   TREATMENT OF WIDOWS[a] OF 1975 COHORT, VARIOUS
EARNINGS LEVELS (1985 DOLLARS DISCOUNTED AT RATE 3 PERCENT
TO 1985)

Division of earnings (Husband-wife)	Total family earnings level (At 1985 wage index)		
	10,000	30,000	50,000
1–0 (single earner)			
P.V. benefits	24,400	46,621	44,594
P.V. taxes[b]	24,503	73,509	85,835
P.V. transfer	−103	−26,888	−41,241
Rate of return	2.99%	1.89%	1.43%
2/3–1/3			
P.V. benefits	20,046	35,117	43,813
P.V. taxes[b]	27,220	81,658	134,642
P.V. transfer	−7,174	−46,541	−90,828
Rate of return	2.20%	0.79%	0.06%
1/2–1/2			
P.V. benefits	20,286	35,792	44,652
P.V. taxes[b]	28,581	85,743	142,905
P.V. transfer	−8,295	−49,951	−98,253
Rate of return	2.08%	0.63%	−0.17%

[a] That is, widows who lose their husbands at age fifty.

[b] Includes taxes paid by husband before his death.

Table 11   RANGE OF ZERO INCREMENTAL RETURN FOR SECOND
EARNERS, WIDOWS, AND DIVORCED WOMEN (1975 COHORT)

First earner's or husband's earnings level	10,000	30,000	50,000
Second earner's or divorced woman's minimum earnings level to receive an incremental return[a]	2,900	9,600	10,000
Widow's minimum earnings level to receive an incremental return[a]	7,600	22,800	26,500
Latest age at which widowhood occurs, and widow first begins work at 2/3 of husband's wage, to receive an incremental return[a]	40	40	42
Latest age at which divorce occurs, and divorced woman first begins work at 2/3 of husband's wage, to receive an incremental return[a]	52	50	55

[a] In this simulation, both earners' wages increase at the male age profile of wages.

the surplus to bail out Medicare, to raise benefits, or to lower taxes. Still, we present these data as if the Social Security Administration's economic and demographic intermediate projections will hold, and the system will have sufficient funds so that tax rates and benefit formulae remain as now scheduled. We also use the current tax law rather than the one about to be phased in.

In Table 9, we first note that the lower dollar figures reflect primarily thirty years of additional discounting. The absolute scale of the system expands, in fact, with increases in average wages. The earnings levels presented have increased with real wages as well, so that a person in this cohort at age forty-five in 2020 will be receiving much higher wages than the 1985 wage index presented here; for example, $30,000 indexed to 1985 would correspond to over $50,000 by 2020. These are still constant 1985 dollars; we choose this way of presenting the data to compare persons of approximately the same position in the income distribution. Note also that the retirement age under current law will have risen from sixty-six to sixty-seven for this cohort relative to the 1945 cohort, that life expectancy has increased substantially, real wages have increased, OASI tax rates are somewhat higher, and the benefits would be taxed at higher tax brackets under the existing income tax (but not under the tax reform about to be passed—whether that will be the tax law in effect when these persons retire is highly unlikely). The pattern of rates of return is quite similar for the different types of families and the different earnings levels. Tables 9 and 10 reflect a similar qualitative pattern, despite the three years of additional discounting making the numbers smaller, to the corresponding Tables 1 and 6. As earnings levels increase, rates of return decrease and lifetime transfers become large negative amounts. As we move from single-earner to two-earner couples, rates of return decline substantially. Comparing Tables 9 and 10, with the same caveats we used when comparing Tables 1 and 6 (the partial ex post nature of treatment of widows who are presumed to survive to age fifty with their husbands), suggests that the rates of return for widows are much lower and the transfers somewhat smaller (including larger negative transfers) than those for the couples in Table 9. The striking feature is that women widowed in middle age are projected to do very poorly under Social Security into the indefinite future under current law.

Table 11, similar to Table 7, but in this case for the 1975 cohort, presents comparable information about the second-earner or divorcee's minimum earnings level to receive incremental returns, the same information for widows, and the latest age at which widowhood or divorce could occur, subject to our assumptions, and any incremental returns to be received on the taxes paid by working widows or divorced women. The pattern is quite similar to that reported in Table 7. Widows need substantial earnings levels to receive any incremental return—that is, to switch from the survivors benefit to their own retired worker benefit. A widow whose husband has received (in 1985 adjusted and indexed dollars) $30,000 per year would have to go back to work at age fifty for the remainder of her work life (assumed to be until age sixty-seven) and earn $22,800 a year in order to receive any incremental return. Similarly, the same woman would have to be widowed no later than age forty if she went back to work at two thirds of her husband's earnings level before she received any incremental return. Analogous data are presented for divorcees and for those with husbands with different earnings levels.

Again, these data reveal the substantial variation in the treatment of divorced and widowed women, depending upon such things as the age at which these events occur, as well as their husbands' or ex-husbands' earnings, and highlight one of the major issues involved in debates over earnings sharing as a possible Social Security reform.

7. Conclusion

We have presented the results of a computer simulation of the expected present value of benefits, taxes, and transfers, and rates of return, and marginal linkage of benefits and taxes for persons in various income levels and family status. The most striking feature is the enormous variation in the treatment, both in total and at the margin, Social Security offers each of these archetypical family types. Perhaps this variation is desirable and warranted; still, it has not been systematically presented as an optimal design for the system, given the magnitude of variation that we have derived.

These results do point out the tremendous amounts at stake for various family types in the Social Security system and any potential reforms in it. Often these amounts dwarf any conceivable changes in tax burdens under the individual income tax. For many groups in the population, the amount of the expected value of the transfers involved exceeds the median value of a home.

Because Social Security is so important, large, and complex, information such as this, despite a history of related studies under earlier actuarial assumptions and law, seems not to have worked its way to the general public discourse concerning the efficiency and equity of the design of the Social Security system. We hope these results will contribute to a better understanding of how the current Social Security retirement system, as it is projected into the future, is likely to affect families of different types and circumstances.

REFERENCES

Auerbach, A. J., and L. J. Kotlikoff. 1985. The efficiency gains from Social Security benefit-tax linkage. NBER Working Paper no. 1645 (June).

Barro, R. J., and M. Feldstein. 1978. The impact of Social Security on private saving: A debate. American Enterprise Institute. Monograph.

Boskin, M. J. 1986. *Too many promises: The uncertain future of Social Security.* Homewood, Ill.: Dow Jones-Irwin.

Boskin, M. J., M. Avrin, and K. Cone. 1983. Modeling alternative solutions to the long-run Social Security funding problem. In *Behavioral simulation methods in tax policy analysis,* ed. M. Feldstein. Chicago: University of Chicago Press.

Boskin, M. J., and L. J. Kotlikoff. 1986. Public debt and United States saving: A new test of the neutrality hypothesis. In *The "new monetary economics," fiscal issues and unemployment,* eds. K. Brunner and A. H. Meltzer. Amsterdam: North-Holland.

Boskin, M. J., L. J. Kotlikoff, D. J. Puffert, and J. B. Shoven. 1986. Social Security: A financial appraisal across and within generations. NBER Working Paper no. 1891. (April).

Boskin, M. J., L. J. Kotlikoff, and J. B. Shoven. 1985. Personal security accounts: A proposal for fundamental Social Security reform. Policy Paper, Center for Economic Policy Research, Stanford University (September).

Boskin, M. J., and J. B. Shoven. 1986. Poverty among the elderly: Where are the holes in the safety net? NBER Working Paper no. 1923 (May).

Burkhauser, R. V., and K. C. Holden, eds. 1982. *A challenge to Social Security: The changing roles of women and men in American society.* New York: Academic Press.

Flowers, M. R. 1977. *Women and Social Security: An institutional dilemma.* Washington, D.C.: American Enterprise Institute.

Hurd, M. D., and J. B. Shoven. 1985. The distributional impact of Social Security. In *Pensions, labor, and individual choice,* ed. D. A. Wise. Chicago: University of Chicago Press.

Lingg, B. A. 1982. Social Security benefits of female retired workers and two-worker couples. *Social Security Bulletin* 45, no. 2 (February).

Pellechio, A. J., and G. P. Goodfellow. 1983. Individual gains and losses from Social Security before and after the 1983 amendments. *Cato Journal* (Fall).

Ricardo-Campbell, R. 1977. *Social Security: Promise and reality.* Stanford: Hoover Institution Press.

Social Security Administration. 1985. Women and Social Security. *Social Security Bulletin* 48, no. 2 (February).

Thompson, L. 1983. The Social Security reform debate. *Journal of Economic Literature* 21, no. 4 (December).